Secret Longings of the Heart

CAROL KENT

Overcoming
Deep Disappointment and
Unfulfilled Expectations

NAVPRESS

BRINGING TRUTH TO LIFE

NavPress Publishing Group
P.O.Box35001, Colorado Springs, Colorado 80935

The Navigators is an international Christian organization. Jesus Christ gave His followers the Great Commission to go and make disciples (Matthew 28:19). The aim of The Navigators is to help fulfill that commission by multiplying laborers for Christ in every nation.

NavPress is the publishing ministry of The Navigators. NavPress publications are tools to help Christians grow. Although publications alone cannot make disciples or change lives, they can help believers learn biblical discipleship, and apply what they learn to their lives and ministries.

© 1990 by Carol J. Kent
All rights reserved. No part of this publication may be reproduced in any form without written permission from NavPress, P.O. Box 35001, Colorado Springs, CO 80935.
Library of Congress Catalog Card Number 90-60917
ISBN 08910-96981

(Originally published as *Secret Passions of the Christian Woman*.)

Cover photo: Mary Kelley

Unless otherwise identified, all Scripture quotations in this publication are from the *Holy Bible: New International Version* (NIV). Copyright © 1973, 1978, 1984, International Bible Society. Used by permission of Zondervan Bible Publishers. Another version used is the *King James Version* (KJV).

Printed in the United States of America

5 6 7 8 9 10 11 12 13 14 15 16 17/99 98 97 96

FOR A FREE CATALOG OF
NAVPRESS BOOKS & BIBLE STUDIES,
CALL 1-800-366-7788 (USA)
or 1-416-499-4615 (CANADA)

CONTENTS

This book is lovingly dedicated to my husband,

Gene Kent

*You are a servant to the emergence of my God-
    given giftedness.*
*You provide hilarious interludes when I take
    my work too seriously.*
*You give of yourself unselfishly to meet the
    needs of others.*
*You are a fun-loving, adventuresome, and
    creative father.*
You enthusiastically support my dreams.
*You are an exciting lover and a stimulating
    conversationalist.*
You challenge me to think.
*You have a passion for God that is demon-
    strated by your actions.*
You are my best friend and I love you.

AUTHOR

Carol Kent is the founder and director of "Speak Up With Confidence" seminars, a ministry committed to helping Christians develop their communication skills.

A member of the National Speakers Association, Carol is a frequent speaker for conferences and retreats throughout the United States and Canada. In addition to conducting the "Speak Up" seminars and speaking for other groups, Carol co-hosts a weekly radio broadcast called "Time Out."

Carol has a B.S. degree in speech education and an M.A. in communication arts from Western Michigan University. She is listed in *Who's Who Among Students in American Universities and Colleges* and was twice selected to appear in *Outstanding Young Women of America*.

Her background includes four years as a drama, speech, and English teacher and two years as director of an Alternative Education Program for Pregnant Teenagers. After a brief time of working as director of women's ministries at a midwestern church, she went into full-time speaking.

Secret Longings of the Heart is Carol's second book. Her first, *Speak Up With Confidence* (Thomas Nelson Publishers, 1987), was recently released in paperback. She has also written *Tame Your Fears* (NavPress, 1993).

Carol and her husband, Gene, live in Port Huron, Michigan. They have a teenage son, Jason. All three enjoy sailing on the Great Lakes in their leisure time.

ACKNOWLEDGMENTS

With deep appreciation and heartfelt gratitude I acknowledge:

My parents, Clyde and Pauline Afman
  You are my constant encouragers and prayer supporters.
  I thank God for your involvement in my ministry.

My son, Jason Paul (J. P.)
  Your effervescent spirit and spontaneous bursts of humor
  kept my heart encouraged during the long hours at the
  computer.

My friend, Deborah K. Jones
  You supported me throughout this project with countless
  hours of personal involvement. Thank you for "praying
  without ceasing," researching, answering my mail, taking
  phone calls, and proofreading the manuscript.

My editor, Traci Mullins
> You taught me the meaning of the word *teamwork*. Coming alongside at a crucial time, you offered fresh ideas, challenging suggestions, and sound structure that gave this project the foundation it needed. In addition to being tremendously gifted as an editor, you had the ability to confront when necessary and to encourage throughout the writing process. Thank you for your friendship and professionalism.

My sisters—Jennie Dimkoff, Paula Tarantino, Bonnie Emmorey, and Joy Carlson
> You provided a combination of laughter, tears, memories, support, and loving encouragement throughout this project. Writing about secret passions of the Christian woman would have been much more difficult without experiencing life with my four *passionate* sisters.

My prayer supporters—Kay Jelinek, Maureen O'Neill, Susanne Rayner, and Marilyn Fenner
> You kept me going when I was tempted to give up. Thank you for supporting me in many tangible ways during the months of writing. You are loved!

PART ONE

PASSIONS: WHAT ARE THEY AND WHERE DO THEY COME FROM?

ONE

HIDDEN LONGINGS OF THE HEART
Recognizing the Passions that Drive Us

*All my longings lie open before you, O Lord; my
sighing is not hidden from you.*
PSALM 38:9

A couple of years ago a friend of mine came for a visit.
Deb is single, goal-oriented, highly motivated, and very creative. During the course of our conversation, she posed a most
intriguing question: "Carol, what makes you weep and pound
the table?"

I was taken aback for a moment. What a strange question.
What *does* make me weep and pound the table? I asked for a
more specific explanation of what she meant.

With growing intensity, she went on: "What do you feel
passionate about?" My mind started spinning. *Passion* was
a word I enjoyed using and secretly thought I possessed,
but now I wasn't even sure I could properly define what it
meant. That day a one-hour lunch with a friend turned into
a four-hour discussion about hopes and dreams, expectations
and disappointments, longings and emotions, inner drives and
resulting actions.

During the course of the afternoon, some heavy-duty brainstorming took place as Deb probed deeply: "What are the *causes, emotions, concerns, problems, people,* and *projects* you feel deeply about?" I soon realized that what I feel deeply about (even on the unconscious level) drastically affects my actions.

She continued, "What does your heart *long* to be involved in? What are your *secret dreams* for the future?" By this time my creativity was flowing and I began communicating at a deeper level, revealing things that passing acquaintances might find too lofty, too imaginative, or even amusing.

After quite some time had passed, I thought the hard questions were over, but I was wrong—Deb was just getting warmed up! "Where are you hurting right now," she asked, "and how does pain affect your perspective?" That was a tough question. I was just coming through a prolonged period of physical pain and my usual optimistic attitude had long since worn thin by the crippling grip of a damaged nerve. My motivation and personal productivity were greatly hindered by my lack of good health, even though my condition was temporary.

Deb's last queries hit me like well-placed bullets and punctured my spiritual conscience. "What are you willing to invest your time, your money, and your total energy toward? What emotions are you feeling that you don't want anyone else to know about?"

Those questions became the springboard for one of the most stimulating discussions I've ever had. There are moments in life when "peak-level" communication takes place and you begin speaking of your secret passions out loud to another human being. That day I revealed my *hidden heartbeat*.

Thinking about hidden passions is one thing. Talking about them is another matter entirely. In addition to my positive, honorable, and spiritual passions, I had to admit I had passions that were stirred by my hurts, failures, family tensions, job problems, personality struggles, secret temptations, deep-felt desires, negative emotions, and bitter disappointments.

Once again I realized that I'm one in millions of women

who struggles with life's complexities. Every day women experience opportunities that have the potential to lift them to glorious, stimulating joy, or plunge them into self-pity and depression. In one twenty-four-hour period, women can shed passionate tears of joy or sob over the loss of a personal relationship or a lost opportunity.

The word *passion* is as complex as the human mind. It's derived from old French and Latin roots, which mean "suffering, pain, or some disorder of body or spirit." I can identify with that! It's also defined as "any kind of *feeling* by which the mind is powerfully affected or moved."[1]

Today, passion has strongly paradoxical meanings. It can mean any one of the emotions (such as hate, grief, love, fear, or joy). It can also refer to an extreme, compelling, emotional drive or excitement, such as: (a) great anger, rage, or fury; (b) enthusiasm or fondness; (c) strong love or affection; or (d) sexual drive or desire, including lust.

For the Christian woman, *passion* also has to do with living for a cause that matters. It's the perspective that no matter what unfair negatives we face, no matter what great personal tragedies come into our lives, *there is something more important to look forward to and to invest our energies toward.* The difference for the Christian woman who passionately desires a more struggle-free life, but never receives it, is that she has an eternal hope which makes momentary troubles more bearable.

WHERE DO SECRET PASSIONS COME FROM?

All of us experience emotional stress and spiritual conflict because of a great dichotomy that stems from birth. These tensions exist because of two basic facts:

Women (and men) are created in the image of God. Genesis 1:27 states, "So God created man in his own image, in the image of God he created him; male and female he created them." Natural man (woman), created in God's image, has tremendous potential—intellectually, artistically, and socially. She has a mind and body fashioned after her Maker's.

As a result, there is an inborn, natural inclination to live as she was created to live—for God's glory, using her individual creativity to make the world a better place and to develop intimate, meaningful relationships with other people. *But . . .*

Sin entered the human race in the Garden of Eden. Eve listened to the serpent's (Satan's) lie and thought she might be missing something wonderful. She ate of the forbidden fruit, a sin that ultimately resulted in (wo)man's separation from God. (Read the complete story in Genesis 3.) Alienation from God seems like very harsh punishment for such a sin. All this trouble brought upon the human race because of *one bite*? What kind of a God would curse the earth and banish His people from paradise because they ate of a little piece of fruit?

All of this makes sense if we understand these things:

- God exists.
- God has a character.
- God's character is holy (totally without sin).
- We are born sinners because of what happened in the Garden of Eden.
- God's sinless character cannot coexist with sinful people.
- For reconciliation to take place between God and man, we must admit we are sinners, agree that sin must be punished, believe Christ's substitutionary death on the cross was sufficient to free us from condemnation, and believe that He rose from the dead.
- To be born into the family of God, we must, by faith, accept all of the above as truth.

WHAT DOES THIS HAVE TO DO WITH MY PASSIONS?

There's a popular advertisement for disposable diapers that uses the Garden of Eden as a setting. The caption reads: IN THE BEGINNING . . . two toddlers wander through the beautiful foliage holding their baby bottles, when the female turns to the male and adoringly offers hers to him, saying, "Want some apple juice?"

When the sin described in Genesis 3 receives such "cute" and positive coverage, it's hard for us to focus on the real problem. *We have a sinful nature at war with our spiritual nature, even after we have accepted Christ as Savior.* We soon discover that our sinful nature tends to pervert and distort our purpose. The sin in our lives (and the sin we see in other people) inevitably leads to the frustration of our highest calling. That calling is to live like Christ, totally free and one with the Father, much like Adam and Eve were *before* the Fall.

This frustration may not be consciously felt, but it nevertheless produces conscious disappointment and pain, which in turn creates a desire for change—personally and in our world. In other words, unfulfilled expectations lead to *disappointment,* which in turn leads to *longings for change* or restoration. Our longings spark *emotion,* which fuels *drive* or *ruling passion.* Ultimately, passion leads to determined *action.*

What are *passions*? A basic definition is, *emotional responses to the disappointment of our expectations.* What determines their power for good or evil is our values system. It is natural to long for change when we are disappointed, but when our passions drive us toward personal relief more than toward honoring God and others, our actions can be destructive.

HOW CAN I CONTROL MY PASSIONS?

There is nothing worse than a sense of being out of control. Most of us want other people to think of us as rational, intelligent, spiritually motivated women who *always* act out our emotions in a controlled, Christlike fashion. But only rarely do we fit that description! Our actions are based on our conscious or unconscious values system and can be positive, godly responses or negative, evil responses.

Understanding the source of our passions and fully recognizing that they are a power source for good or evil will help us make some key decisions. We need to establish a values system that can "take the heat" and help us to make right choices, even though passions are major forces within us.

How does this work? My friend Ginny's experience provides a good illustration.

Ginny's Story

"I had already planned the murder in my mind. I knew *exactly* how I would execute it. I wanted to inflict pain. I wanted to mutilate. I wanted to kill. I wanted to *destroy* the man who hurt my daughters. I would have carried out my plan and I'd be in prison today if two thousand miles had not separated me from Jim."

In total shock I looked across the table at my friend. Her face was familiar, but everything else was different. My mind suddenly flashed back to school days when I remembered sitting at my desk, taking an IQ test. Across the top of the page, big letters spelled out the instructions: WHAT'S WRONG WITH THIS PICTURE?

My head was spinning. I hadn't seen Ginny for several years and I could hardly believe what she was saying. Prior to this conversation, if I'd been asked to list the most gentle, sensitive, loving Christian women I'd ever met, Ginny would have been on the list. Now my mind scrambled to recall Ginny's incredible story of survival. I knew her ex-husband, Jim, had been very physically abusive, especially when he had been drinking. She never talked much about Jim, but her terrible fear of this man had been obvious to close friends. Ginny had been battered physically and verbally on numerous occasions, but she stayed with her husband, praying for a miracle.

For fifteen years she had tried to salvage what was left of the marriage. Ginny felt false pride and shame about the stubborn decision she had made to marry this man. She feared divorce would affect her relationship with God. But there were two young daughters to protect. One day while Jim was in a drunken rage, he lunged at her with a knife in his hand; she knew then it was time to leave and take her precious daughters with her. After the divorce, I rarely heard Ginny complain in spite of heavy financial and emotional struggles.

She honestly admitted her deep loneliness and frustrations with single parenting, but her faith seemed unshakable.

Ginny's voice brought me back to the present. "You know, Carol, my daughters are grown now. They are beautiful, compassionate, and intelligent young women, and they have brought me joy even during the most discouraging days of my life. Last year they flew in to visit me. While the girls were in town, we were invited to have dinner in the home of dear friends. Following the meal, our conversation turned to past events and future goals; we shared openly and then we went on to a time of prayer."

Struggling to control her emotions, Ginny continued her story. "During the prayer time, both of my girls began weeping uncontrollably. I put my arms around them and one of them said, 'Mom, we can't keep the secret any longer. We feel so dirty. Can God ever forgive us? After your divorce from Daddy, when it was his weekend to have us, he would drink and then force himself on Jody and me. He had sex with us almost every time it was his turn for visitation. Maybe we could have stopped him, but we didn't know what to do. We love Dad, but he was always so different when he was drinking. We feel like we've sinned against God. Will we ever quit feeling so dirty?'"

Ginny paused, and with fire in her eyes she stated, "Carol, until that moment I didn't know I was capable of feeling such an intense level of hatred. Every cell in my body was screaming relentlessly. Anger and desire for vengeance flooded over me as I comprehended the reality of my worst fear: My little girls, who were only ten and eleven years old at the time, had been repeatedly sexually abused by their own father! Sexual abuse—what a hideous phrase! Rage seared through my veins, but this time it was directed at God. Where was He when this happened? Couldn't He have stopped it?"

Ginny took a deep breath and explained more of this horror story. While listening to her girls that night, she mentally devised a plan for killing the man who had brought her children such heartfelt pain and undeserved guilt.

Ginny spoke haltingly as she related the story of her

lengthy personal battle to forgive her ex-husband for such a heinous crime. She carried intense anger at God for a full year. She hated the dryness in her relationship with the Lord, but her disappointment and anger outweighed her desire for change. One day, with her emotions warring within, she fell to her knees. By faith, not feeling, she poured her heart out to God. Jody and Karen were beside her and she voiced her prayer aloud.

"Dear God," Ginny began. "In myself I cannot speak the words, but in Your strength I ask for help. Lord, *by faith* I forgive Jim for sexually abusing my young daughters and for making them live with such a horrible guilt-producing secret all of these years. Father, I cannot do this apart from You. Take away the guilt and the hatred. Free my girls from the painful memories of the past. Replace this horror with Your love. Give them healing and mental rest. Grant them spiritual wholeness. Forgive me for my wicked, murderous thoughts toward this man. Oh, God, I thank You for hearing me today and for giving me Your peace. Amen."

How Ginny Controlled Her Passions

Ginny's story does not have an ending yet. I have not told her story for the purpose of offering a quick-fix solution or to suggest that deeply hidden passions—such as murderous thoughts—can be instantly controlled with one sincere prayer. None of us will experience the absence of all pain until we reach Heaven. To pretend that hurt isn't there or that life is perfect "now that we're right with God" would be to deny that we live in a fallen world with unfulfilled longings, disappointments, abuse, lust, hunger, pain, confusion, and at times more questions than answers.

But if we look more closely at what happened in Ginny's mind and heart as she responded to her circumstances, we can see a clear process at work that enabled her to redirect her murderous impulses.

Ginny's Expectation: That she would have a happy Christian marriage and would raise two lovely daughters in a positive environment until they were able to be on their own as productive, contributing members of society.

Ginny's Disappointment: Her marriage was a failure and her daughters were sexually abused by their own father. Consequently, her daughters had the potential of being negatively affected for life in their personal relationships.

Ginny's Longing: This great disappointment stirred a mixture of deep longings within Ginny for change or restoration. One longing was that she and her daughters would *never* have to see Jim again and that he would never be allowed to see them again. Another longing was an intense desire to protect her daughters and to "fix" any damage that had been done to them.

Ginny's Emotion: Her longings immediately brought violent emotions; in this case, anger and hatred directed at Jim that resulted in murderous thoughts. She wanted to inflict slow, agonizing pain with the same intensity she and her daughters had experienced.

Ginny's Decision: Up until this point, Ginny's responses were morally neutral. But a decision had to be made regarding what to do with those negative emotions. Since there was a great physical distance between her and her ex-husband, Ginny spent a considerable amount of time sifting her poignant feelings through the grid of her personal convictions. Ginny is a Christian who has a strong system of values based on the Bible. After she analyzed her sharply painful emotions in the light of her relationship with God, her knowledge of His Word, and her intense love for her daughters, the decision finally was made.

Ginny's Drive/Passion: If she had valued relief more than anything else, Ginny's drive (ruling passion) would have been revenge. That passion would have produced vengeful action toward Jim—possibly even murder! But Ginny made a different—though difficult—decision. Above all else she valued obeying God and becoming like Christ, and she knew God's will was for her to forgive. Her ruling passion, therefore, resulted in an action of Christlike behavior.

Ginny's Action: When a decision is made regarding a ruling passion, the final action will be directed toward good or evil. For Ginny, the action of prayer was required, asking God for the grace to develop and display forgiveness in her life.

If Ginny had not stopped to consider her values in the light of God's, or if she had denied what she most deeply longed for (which actually was to be God's woman), she might have let her natural, sinful bent toward evil drive her to destruction. One of her major longings was to protect her daughters and help them to be emotionally healed. After considering her deep desire to choose to be God's woman, her fiery passion cooled in an action of forgiveness and an ongoing involvement in nurturing her daughters.

LET'S GET HONEST

This is a book about facing secret passions. Each chapter will identify a different hidden longing that—consciously or unconsciously—fuels our passions. Many different longings provide kindling for the fire of passions. We have longings *to possess* things that are out of our reach. We experience longings *to escape* difficult life situations. Some of us deeply desire *to transform* our lives from the inside out. Others of us want *to transcend* daily circumstances and live out our real purpose. And all of us long *to matter* to somebody else, to feel significant.

Our longings can result in ruling passions and actions that are twisted, honorable, or holy. This book is written for women who desire to learn the secret of handling the disappointment of their unfulfilled expectations in the right way so their ruling passions will be powerful forces for good rather than evil.

The requirements for getting the most out of this book are rigorous honesty and a careful response to the following questions:

- What are the aches in my heart that have never been touched?
- Do I have hidden, negative emotions that have been covered over with denial or feverish work?

- Is there anyone I dislike, hate, envy, resent, or fear?
- What are my secrets?
- Do I understand God's answers to my hidden longings?
- Am I living for a purpose that transcends my daily routine and problems?
- What are my expectations of myself and my world?
- How do I usually handle my disappointments?

Why should we be in touch with the deepest parts of ourselves? The greatest benefit is that we can begin making conscious, God-honoring decisions about our present and our future, rather than being driven blindly by our emotions. In the next chapter we'll get started by evaluating our own longings, which fuel the passions behind our actions.

TWO

SECRET PASSIONS—TWISTED, HONORABLE, OR HOLY?
Recognizing the Sources of Passion

I turned my mind to understand, to investigate and to search out wisdom.
ECCLESIASTES 7:25

All of us have passions. These drives, fed by our longings, are often kept in a secret place, far from the knowledge of other people—and even ourselves. Sometimes these secret passions are fueled by strong negative emotions, such as Ginny experienced when she was filled with hurt and anger over the abuse of her daughters. When the emotion rages, the secret passion becomes common knowledge as actions are carried out.

Passions can be based on a deep longing to escape from our present circumstances. Or they can be produced by an intense desire to have something out of reach. Passion is the fuel that produces major changes in our lifestyle, behavior, and attitudes. Ultimately, passions can give us the energy to live out our real purpose in life and see the big picture.

Occasionally secret passions are fiercely spiritual. These passions drive us to work for a creed, cause, or desired outcome that is high and holy. These kinds of passions are often based on our longings to live out the purpose we were created for and to use our best gifts for a worthy cause.

HOW DO UNCONSCIOUS PASSIONS DRIVE US?

Life goes by at a very fast pace. Our days are filled with making a living, interacting with people, responding to emergencies, fulfilling obligations, keeping pace with current demands, eating, sleeping, and personal hygiene. That leaves very little time to stop long enough to think about *why* we do what we do.

A young woman told me she had struggled for the past four years with a severe eating disorder. She explained her cycle of binging on enormous amounts of food, then purging through inducing vomiting and abusing laxatives. Lori was slender, attractive, and educated. My first thought was, *Why would someone like this have a problem like that?*

After a while I asked, "Lori, do you know why you first started this cycle of binging and purging?"

She immediately responded. "Because I wanted to look good to other people. It was simply a way of controlling my weight when I desired food that had too many calories. I guess I felt I had no self-control."

As we moved deeper into the discussion, she told me her mother had always been substantially overweight and her father used to joke about her fat in demeaning ways, often in front of other people. He would frequently pinch her mother's extra flesh along the ribs or move her saggy, heavy arms back and forth while making derogatory comments. Lori always felt like crying when this happened; but to her dad, it was always a humorous matter.

Lori's father was demanding in many ways; she was afraid to bring home her report card for fear he would be disappointed with a "B+" grade instead of an "A." He was slow to praise, and even as a young adult Lori admitted she was still trying to be good enough to please him.

It soon became obvious to me why Lori had severe bulimia. Her present dilemma had resulted from a series of subconscious decisions, based on disappointed longings that fed her passion and finally produced destructive action. Let's take a look at how it happened.

Lori's Expectation: That her father would love her, affirm her, and be pleased with her; that he would love, verbally affirm, and be pleased with her mother.

Lori's Disappointment: Through the years, no matter how hard her mother tried to please her husband (Lori's father), he was still relentless with his hurtful criticism. Likewise, Lori discovered it was impossible to do anything well enough to earn her father's approval.

Lori's Longing: Her deep disappointment led to a desire for change. In Lori's case, her true longing was for unbridled, unearned, pure, nonjudgmental, Christlike love from her father that would be directed toward her and her mother, regardless of their physical appearance or performance. This longing was not fully understood by Lori, and she continued to try to find a way to be acceptable to her dad.

Lori's Emotions: Lori's emotions included a *zeal* to be thin enough to win her father's acceptance and a *fear* of ridicule, embarrassment, and rejection if she ever became overweight.

Lori's Decision: She knew (intellectually) that God loved her and she was important to Him no matter how much she weighed, but her values system had become distorted by years of unsuccessfully trying to please her father and by watching her mother crumble under his incessant criticism. The damage to her emotions and thinking processes made relief (soothing her pain by controlling her body) her highest priority—and her actions reflected that choice.

Lori's Drive/Passion: If Lori's values had been tied securely to the authority of God's Word, if she'd been convinced of her unalterable worth to her Father in Heaven, her ruling passion could have become devotion to Him. She could have chosen to accept His unconditional love and protection and experience worth as His child rather than attempting to meet her earthly father's expectations (and her desire for relief from the pain of his disapproval). Because her values were unclear and her deepest longings unacknowledged, her instinctive drive was to be physically attractive—no matter what the cost.

Lori's Action: The cost for Lori was bondage to a severe eating disorder.

She had tried several diets even though she was not overweight. When she discovered it was difficult to take off an additional five pounds, she tried something new. One day, while watching a television talk show, she was introduced to people who had eating disorders. Instead of grasping the show's message that eating disorders are severe problems requiring attention, Lori focused on the testimony of one guest who said she lost a huge amount of weight by purging and using laxatives. Lori had never heard of this before, so she decided to try it. Now, four years later, she felt hopelessly addicted to a behavior that was controlling her social life and paralyzing her spiritual life.

SECRET PASSIONS

Our secret passions have their roots in deep longings within—desires we think about regularly but often avoid declaring openly. Most of us don't talk about our secret passions, since we're convinced no one else could possibly empathize with our unique situation in life. On the other hand, sometimes we only *fear* that someone won't understand, or we worry that our secret will be handled carelessly or without compassion. It's often easier for us to hide our true feelings than to risk rejection or ridicule.

These hidden passions are also formed by the subconcious longings we are too busy to recognize or too hurt to admit. Sometimes we're aware of our longings but not in touch with the emotions they spark. If Lori had known she longed for her father's approval, but wasn't aware how hurt, angry, fearful, and even ashamed she felt over not receiving approval, then knowing her longings wouldn't have done her any good. So it's vital that we understand the connection between our longings and our emotions that lead us to action.

Hidden passions are difficult to direct as a power source for good, because it's much easier to exist in a comfortable rut rather than risking vulnerability and talking to someone about our personal need. *By not being in touch with our longings and emotions, we lose the ability to make conscious decisions about our present and future and end up living by our emotions.*

Hidden longings reveal the *real* person inside of us as they feed the passions that drive us. According to Proverbs 23:7 (KJV), "As [a man] thinketh in his heart, so is he."

Knowing such a powerful force lies within us provides powerful motivation for us to understand the longings that feed our passions. Who is the "real person" inside of us? Sometimes we're afraid to acknowledge our longings and emotions because we're afraid to face that real person inside. But the truth is, we are passionate people, full of potential for good and evil. What we need is a power greater than ourselves—a power that will enable us to channel our passions in a positive direction.

PASSIONS—TWISTED, HONORABLE, OR HOLY?

In the first chapter we mentioned that our ruling passions (or drives) are determined by our values system and can be characterized any of the following three ways.

Twisted

Twisted passions destroy a person's potential for happiness, personal productivity, and spiritual fulfillment.

Example one: A Christian mother expects that her son will one day become an adult with an opportunity for marriage, a good job, and a family. Her son is killed at age sixteen by a drunk driver. This mother longs to have her son back. Since that isn't possible, her longing for change turns to the driver of the vehicle. She wants him to pay for what he did by serving time in prison and having his driver's license removed permanently. This mother's initial emotion is anger toward the driver and a deep desire for revenge. Thoughts of God are far from her at the moment. With a distorted values system, she makes her decision. Her ruling passion becomes an intense drive to constantly relive the details of the accident and verbalize fitting punishments for the driver. Her twisted action makes the people around her miserable. The result for this woman is bitterness, poor health, and depression; but she does not view her passion as a sin or a problem needing attention.

Example two: A Christian woman has an expectation that marriage will provide security and significance. Her expectation comes from her inner knowledge that she was created to live in a perfect, pre-fallen world. She winds up with a difficult marriage on many levels—no meaningful communication, intimacy, or financial security. She longs for a fulfilling marriage and becomes increasingly frustrated and depressed when her situation doesn't change. Because she values being rid of emotional pain more than anything else, the passion of lust is fueled, and she ends up in an affair with a married man as an "anesthetic" to bring emotional relief.

Honorable
Honorable passions result in bringing energy and enthusiasm to uplifting and worthwhile relationships, causes, and projects.

Example one: Another woman with an equally difficult marriage has a high expectation that her marriage will be a Christ-centered union of two people with mutual spiritual goals. After a brief honeymoon, the marriage crumbles and every expectation this wife has for the perfect Christian union is shattered.

She has thought deeply about what beliefs and values are worth living for, and more than anything she wants to be God's channel of love in this world—in spite of the cost. She longs to have her needs met in marriage, but even more she longs to fulfill her purpose in the world: to love God and others. Because her values are godly, her passions become godly. Her disappointment ultimately fuels the passion of love, a love that is willing to live through the painful process of building a good marriage, if that is even possible. Her passion directs her to show that love creatively as God directs. Both the woman whose passion ended in an affair and this woman have conflicting emotions at times, but their values always determine their *ruling* passion.

Example two: A young woman had a sister who was born with cystic fibrosis. She watched as her sister Dayna struggled with a terminal illness that allowed her enough healthy periods to significantly impact her world with numerous personal contributions. Dayna blessed others with her contagious sense of humor, watercolor paintings, challenging conversation, and deep loyalty in friendships. Serious symptoms of the disease periodically flared up with no advance notice, leaving Dayna with severe breathing and digestive problems. When Dayna died, her passing seemed premature. There were so many things she wanted to accomplish, so many hopes and dreams left unfulfilled.

Her sister, propelled by a passion that had God's interests at heart, took up the cause of making the Cystic Fibrosis Foundation a major focus of her energy. Instead of wasting precious time mourning indefinitely for a sister who was gone, she devoted several hours a week to fund-raising and making speeches that motivated the search for a cure for this dreadful disease.

Holy

Holy passions bring about fulfillment of the Great Commission—leading people to Christ and leading young Christians to maturity through instruction.

Example one: A. Wetherell Johnson, an English-born missionary to China, was put in a Japanese internment camp near Shanghai during World War II. When released, she was in poor health and was robbed of her former place of ministry. Already in her fifties, she went to California to recuperate.

Instead of settling into retirement with every possibility of feeling bitter and resentful for being thrown into a prison camp, thrust out of a mission field, and besieged with poor health, she saw a new opportunity to minister to a handful of women. She started a home Bible study that soon moved to a church because of the number of women who came. People in other cities asked her to start Bible studies in their areas, and within a few short years Miss Johnson founded what is now called Bible Study Fellowship.

Today, thousands of men and women study her Bible study notes in weekly classes held around the globe. Countless people have been won to Christ and receive regular instruction from the Word of God as a result of one woman's holy passion.

Upon release from the prison camp, Miss Johnson stated, "Your deepest joy comes when you have nothing around you to bring outward pleasure and Jesus becomes your total joy."[1] Miss Johnson's values determined how she handled her disappointments and they became the energy behind her holy passion.

Example two: Jill left her nursing position at the hospital when her husband received a raise and asked her to quit work so they could spend more time together. Even though they didn't need the income, her expectation had always been that she would help people through nursing. Her disappointment at the thought of leaving the job she loved was intense. Jill struggled with her emotions for a while, feeling angry at her husband for his unwavering position that she quit her job.

Because of her Christian values system (and the prayers of dear friends), Jill came to channel her emotions toward deep love, not only for her husband, but for others. Her passionate love for helping people opened a door for her to volunteer her services once a week at a local convalescent home. In addition to using her nursing skills, she held a Bible study once a week, and within a year, five people came to know Christ as a result of hearing the gospel during these sessions. She soon realized her current "job" was much more fulfilling than the one she left, and she still had ample time to spend with her husband.

WHAT LONGINGS ARE BURIED IN YOUR HEART?

My interest in this subject comes from an inner knowledge that my personal passions control me. When they are honorable and holy, wonderful things happen. People around me are encouraged and I have an inner sense of joy and deep personal fulfillment.

The problem is that more often than I'd like to admit, my passions are twisted. The reason for this is that when I dwell on my disappointments and the reality that certain things in life aren't what I expect, I long for a change. And sometimes my longings are so intense that I react solely from my emotions. I don't stop to think about what God values or how my goals line up with His. My emotions, rather than my values, drive me—sometimes toward destruction.

I've always been curious about why I do what I do. What drives me? Why do I work so hard for approval? Why do my disappointments spur me toward deep longings for change? If you're like me, you probably ask yourself some of the same questions.

I don't think deeply each day about what determines my actions, but I instinctively know when my behavior and attitudes are God-honoring or when they are twisted. My biggest purpose in writing this book is to help people like me understand how to recognize the longings that lead to passions, and to recognize them in time to control the emotions and choose the action that will exalt the Lord and help other people. We can't do it alone, but with prayer, practice, and patience, there is hope!

When the idea for this book first came to me, I began interviewing women all across the country about their secret passions. Their gut-level honesty and surprisingly frank responses to my questions helped me to identify certain kinds of longings that form the bedrock of passion—passion that can be constructive or destructive, concealed or celebrated. In each case, there is a choice. Will the action that is motivated by the longing be twisted, honorable, or holy?

Maybe you, like me, have experienced some of the same disappointments that produce the following five types of longings. (It's somehow comforting to think that I might not be alone in my struggle to direct my longings in the right direction.)

In the following examples, the places, names, and a few significant details are changed to protect the anonymity of the individuals who shared their stories. As you read each story, ask yourself what longings are buried in your heart and how your longings have produced your ruling passions.

FIVE TYPES OF LONGINGS

Longing to Matter (to have impact and significance)
• "I was the fifth daughter born in my family. From the time I was very small, it was obvious that my father had been wanting a son—probably since the first girl was born. Two years later he got his wish and my brother was born. Dad played ball with Billy and took him hunting. There were lots of baby pictures of Billy, but almost none of me. Even though my basic needs of food, clothing, and shelter were met, I never felt special to my father. All my life I've wanted him to be proud of me and to enjoy spending time with me, but that's never happened."

• "For years I have been calling a woman regularly to talk about all my troubles and to ask for her advice. I would like to have her as a friend, but I don't feel good enough about myself to feel worthy of that kind of a relationship. I'm really afraid that if I didn't have personal struggles and concerns to bring up on the phone, she'd wonder why someone like me would be calling her."

Longing to Possess (to have something out of reach)
• "All I have ever wanted is a baby of my own. I have had five miscarriages, and every time I see a happy mother holding her tiny infant, part of me cries and the other part gets angry at God. *Why* would He withhold from me that which I want most? It isn't fair!"

• "I'll turn forty this year and my husband and I have never owned a home of our own. We have worked harder than most couples; we've always tried to budget, but we have *never* been out of debt. Last year the car fell apart and had to be replaced. This year we had unexpected medical expenses.

There's always something that keeps us from our deep longing for financial security, and the stress is more than I can bear."

• "I'm trapped in a body with cerebral palsy. My mind is like yours, but my muscles won't work properly. How would you like to sit in a restaurant and have the waitress ask if it's *safe* to put silverware in front of you? People assume I'm mentally retarded because they don't understand my disability. I long for physical wholeness, but in this lifetime I will not get my wish."

• "When God made me, He must have run out of good building material. I have exercised with Jane Fonda for the last three years, but I'm still too short, too round, and too plain. No diet I've ever tried has removed my fat tummy and my chunky thighs. My skin is pitted from teenage acne, and I have never felt beautiful for even one day of my life."

• "Every day I ask God for a husband, and I haven't had a date in two years. I long for someone to hold me tenderly. I'm not asking for a Don Johnson or a Robert Redford. A regular, average, kind, loving man would do. I am so lonely I could die."

• "I was passed over for the position I'm most qualified for, and now I'm stuck in a dead-end job that requires none of my creativity. I'm bored, unhappy, depressed, and unfulfilled. I need my paycheck for survival and see no hope for getting out of the rut."

Longing to Escape (to be released from bondage)
• "I married the best-looking guy in the world! He was the strong, silent type and there was something about his slow speech that gave him an aura of mystery and intrigue. Now we've been married for ten years and I'm wondering why. This man refuses to carry on a conversation. If he isn't buried in the newspaper, he's totally engrossed in a television sports event. He never speaks to me of what happens at the office, and we haven't had a meaningful discussion about our hopes and dreams for the future since before we were married. He will not communicate, and he has no concept of how cut-off I feel. I wish there was a way to gracefully leave this marriage and find

someone to give me the companionship my heart desires."

• "Working in my profession is one of the opportunities of a lifetime! It's fulfilling, challenging, mentally and spiritually stimulating, and they *pay* me to do it. The only trouble is that the more I work, the more there is to do. My work possesses my mind from the moment I get up to the minute I lie down. I wake up in the night and can't get back to sleep because creative ideas are swirling in my head. My husband and son are constantly trying to break me out of a preoccupied daze by saying, 'Earth to Mother! Earth to Mother!' I seem incapable of *balancing* my life so that my inner drive to accomplish 'important' work is kept in proper perspective without holding me in bondage to it."

• "My greatest internal struggle is with my fantasies. I long to be cherished, and my husband isn't meeting that need. When I meet charming Christian men, I inevitably think about being in their arms and making love with someone who would make me feel beautiful and desirable. I have confessed this sin to God repeatedly, but the thoughts always come back."

• "If I could be released from anger, I could be a good Christian woman. My mother has been overprotective since the day I was born. She never allowed me to make my own decisions, and she saw my emerging independence as a threat. Now I'm in my mid-thirties and she's still controlling my life. Just last week she told me to quit wearing eye shadow because it makes me look like a prostitute. I can't believe she is *still* capable of reducing me to tears and manipulating my emotions like this. I'm tired of being hurt, criticized, and humiliated in front of others. Just seeing her enter a room makes me so angry I could scream!"

• "I long for Heaven. I've lived enough years to understand how short our time is on earth. My husband went home to be with the Lord five years ago, and I'm looking forward to eternity myself. My body is racked with arthritis. I'm in pain when I wake up; I'm in pain when I move; I'm in pain when I go to bed. How long will I have to suffer before I can go home, too?"

Longing to Transform (to change from the inside out)
• "While I'm smiling on the outside, I'm struggling with jealousy on the inside. So many women have an easier life than I do, and envy is starting to take root. Each day I mentally list what I dislike about my circumstances and I'm always wishing I could be confident and happy like other people."

• "I was born with a negative attitude. In spite of being raised in a good home with encouraging parents, I have always tended to criticize before praising. Sometimes I can't believe the harsh tone of my voice and the demeaning speech that comes out of my mouth. I wish I could be a more positive person."

**Longing to Transcend (to see
the bigger picture and live out my real purpose)**
• "There's a spiritual dimension to my life that longs to make a tangible difference in this world. When I read stories of moral injustice in the world, I'm ready to sign a petition or to make a speech to defend the just and to stand up for what's right. I have a burning passion to see the Supreme Court decision on abortion reversed. If it means money, time, or personal commitment, I will do whatever it takes to bring the truth to the forefront and to defend innocent victims."

• "My husband and I live in a house with mud walls and a mud floor. When we married I didn't know that we would become missionaries in Bolivia. The roaches are so big here; they began eating up our wedding gifts. The heat, humidity, and bugs are often our greatest discouragements, but we are driven by one supreme desire—to bring the message of salvation to the native tribes of Bolivia. We will not give up because our eye is on the goal of reaching men and women with the truth of God's love."

THE NEXT STEP

One of the first steps to Christian growth is to identify our hidden longings. Are they drawing us closer to God or pulling us away from Him? The next few chapters will help us explore our inner chambers. Each of us has deep longings for significance, security, intimacy, success, and spirituality. Is that wrong?

Absolutely not! God knows our longings and the emotions they spark, and He understands them. It was God Himself who placed pre-Fall expectations and desires in our hearts, and He doesn't condemn us for having feelings. He also understands the personal process we go through as we develop the passions that rule our lives, and He is always ready and willing to help us sort out our secret feelings and thoughts—even the ones that don't seem "right."

When we *own* our personal passions and stand before Him, all pretense is dropped and one by one we can evaluate our inner longings, emotions, and motives in the light of His holiness. That sounds like a big order, but God wants us to recognize our passions for what they are, acknowledge their potential power, and channel them for good instead of evil.

It's very motivating for me to realize that my secret passions can be a tremendous source of power for getting God's work accomplished in this world. By acknowledging and evaluating our passions, we can discover how to lead a much more honest, focused, fulfilling, and purposeful life—a life based on eternal values.

Instead of feeling ashamed or threatened by our emotions, we can pass them through the grid of a values system based on the Word of God, so our passions and ultimately our actions will be for our good, the good of others, and the good of God's Kingdom. I really want that to be true in my life, and it all starts with gut-level honesty. Let's get started!

PART TWO

THE PASSION FOR SIGNIFICANCE

THREE

I WANT TO FEEL SPECIAL
To Know Whose I Am

I'm Nobody! Who are you? Are you—Nobody—too?
Then there's a pair of us! Don't tell! They'd
advertise—you know.
EMILY DICKINSON, 1861

Empty. Alone. Hurting. I could see the young woman out of the corner of my eye. She was strategically moving through the crowd toward me, pressing against clumps of people gathered into randomly placed conversation clusters in the small room. Her sallow, anxious face told a story without words. She had problems in her life, and she wanted to talk to somebody—anybody who would listen.

Glancing at the clock and knowing time pressures were great, I discreetly scanned the room for the closest exit. By moving quickly, I could safely remove myself from the possibility of getting into a lengthy discussion with the nameless woman. Turning to go, I found myself face-to-face with an eager conference participant. She bubbled with enthusiasm and thanked me for speaking. After chatting momentarily, I proceeded toward the door to make my escape.

Within two feet of freedom, I felt a tug on my arm. Turning

around, my eyes momentarily met those of my pursuer. She haltingly stammered, "I know you probably don't have much time, but could we talk for a moment before you leave? In your message today. . . ." She hesitated again, trying to express her thoughts. I could feel myself pulling away, stepping slowly toward the door, avoiding serious eye contact, and casually glancing at my watch while simultaneously feigning interest in this woman's need.

She read my body language as easily as if it had been shouted through a megaphone. Backing off, she mumbled, "Oh, never mind. I know you're busy. It was nothing anyway. Thank you for coming today."

Caught! Guilty! Convicted! The words were reverberating like a hammer in my conscience, reminding me that my subtle "pulling away" from this woman had just negated everything I had said in my presentation about how significant we are to God and how, in turn, we should practice the example of Jesus.

I had carefully reminded the listeners of the necessity to look closely at the life of Christ recorded in the gospels and notice the way He responded to people. When He looked at individuals, He had kind eyes and empathy. He had a way of looking people in the eye and nonverbally communicating that they were important, valued, and singly significant.

And He touched them. I described Him moving through the crowds with focused eye contact, picking out people who were lonely and felt unworthy, and reaching out with a touch to communicate hope and love to them.

I had carefully pointed out that everywhere He went, Jesus gave people a sense of identity and worthiness. He practiced body language that made people feel accepted and special. Throughout the gospels we read that *Jesus looked at people with eyes of compassion,* and *He touched them.*

Stabbed with a pang of guilt, I went after the woman and found a quiet place to talk. I was initially surprised by her lack of focused eye contact. For someone who had desired this meeting so much, she appeared unable to look at me for longer than an instant; then her gaze would go to the floor, to her lap, or to the wall. Without words, her behavior made a strong statement. She had no self-worth, and it had been a monumental act of courage for her to approach me.

She spoke with measured caution. "I'm Meg. I'm nobody special, and I shouldn't be taking your time; but I had to talk to somebody. . . ."

THE BASIC TRUTH

I was born with a need to feel significant. You were, too! We need to know that we are important to someone else. If you were born in a home where your worth was questioned, you have no doubt struggled for a lifetime trying to discover a sense of *belonging*.

If, however, you were told from your earliest days that you are a uniquely special human being, you may feel good about yourself. The real problem is that most of us question our worth regularly, even if we had the most positive upbringing. We need to be told *daily* that somebody out there cares about us.

Perhaps because *feeling significant* is a lifelong battle for most of us—even for mature Christian women—we have an urgent need to know beyond any doubt that we are personally important to God, and He has something important for us to do with our time, talent, and energy.

As I already mentioned in the first chapter of this book, the Bible gives us a clear statement of our worth. Genesis 1:27 says, "So God created man in his own image, in the image of God he created him; male and female he created them." Francis Schaeffer put it this way, "God tells man who he is. God tells us that He created man in His image. So man is something wonderful."[1]

Psalm 139 tells us that we are fearfully and wonderfully made. We are reminded that God created our inmost being and knit us together in our mother's womb. We're told that our frame was not hidden from God when we were formed in the secret place and that His eyes saw our unformed body. The psalmist also states that all of the days that God ordained for us were written in His book before we were even born.

So why do we so often question our worth? Why do feelings of insignificance sometime cloud everything the Bible says about us? Why do we sometimes let one person destroy our sense of belonging? Why do we struggle with what other people think of us? Is it *really* that important?

Ethel Barrett wrote, "We would worry less about what others think of us if we realized how seldom they do!"[2] That's very humbling, but the truth is we *do* care what other people think of us! We read their nonverbal language when we enter a room. If they flash us a smile and greet us with open, warm gestures, we feel valuable and accepted. If they're busy with someone else and take no time to acknowledge our presence, we question our worth and tend to withdraw.

Meg's Story

The woman I mentioned earlier had a story to tell. That day Meg shared her heart with me. She was the fifth daughter born to her parents. Two years later her father, who had longed for a son, got his wish. The day of her brother's birth, her father came bursting into the house saying, "It's a boy! It's a boy! After all these years, I have a son!" During the Christmas holidays that year, the family sent a special picture card to friends and relatives with news of the birth.

Meg's sister, Susan—child number four—was especially attractive. While Meg was young, she would often hear her parents say to guests, "Yes, Susan is the little beauty in the family."

The words stung, and Meg decided to compensate in her own way. She might not have been born beautiful, but she was smart and excelled in school. Her grades were high. Susan, on the other hand, struggled with her schoolwork. When Meg's parents saw the respective report cards, they withheld from Meg any words of affirmation, praise, or approval for her outstanding grades. They feared Susan would feel bad and praise might make Meg become too full of pride.

The family picture albums confirmed to Meg that she was the unwanted child. There was an abundance of pictures of her brother, and there were numerous photos of her older sisters at play, but almost none of Meg.

During the next few years, Meg practiced two opposing lifestyles on an intermittent basis. For a number of years, she was a workaholic, striving for top grades and scholarships, desperately seeking significance through earning the approval her heart desired. When no approval was shown, she turned inward, withdrawing from family and friends. With so many children to care for, Meg's parents didn't notice the obvious signals. They never realized how hurt and angry she was becoming. Meg made her own mental outline: (1) She was unwanted, (2) she was ugly, (3) she was shy, and (4) she wished she'd never been born.

Meg watched as her father lovingly affirmed her older sisters; he was also quick to put an arm around her brother and support him by attending all of his softball games. But when Meg received the lead part in her junior play and had practiced for months, her mother came to the production alone. Her father excused himself, saying he couldn't attend because the play was the same night as his church board meeting. Meg was gracious on the outside, but fiery emotions of deep anger and intense hurt were building on the inside like a volcano.

By the time I met Meg, she had quit school, given birth to a child out of wedlock, married a man who beat her, and had no contact with her parents. Her sense of worth was so low she found it impossible to hold her head up. She slumped like a shapeless piece of clay in the chair beside me. So far from God. So hopeless. So sad. No anticipation for the future. No sense of belonging. No knowledge of worthiness. A lone tear aimlessly made its way down her cheek to the corner of her mouth. I groped for words. There was nothing in me that could quote Bible verses, pray a meaningful prayer, or tell her things would get better when she got right with God.

My own emotions were compassion and concern for the woman I'd tried to flee from one hour earlier. I put my arms around her and wept like a baby, only to find that she stiffened beneath my touch. Physical touch from a caring human being was foreign to her, and she felt uncomfortable receiving it.

Could she ever know how special she was to God if her own father had never given her a sense of belonging?

UNDERSTANDING LOW SELF-ESTEEM

Meg's situation is more severe than some of us go through, but there is not a woman alive who does not understand what it feels like to be a "nobody." The universal struggle for all of us is a deep, painful yearning to know that there is *something* about us that *somebody* finds special. Physical beauty and financial security do little to keep the doubts from coming. And feeling significant for a moment in time does nothing to guarantee that questions of worth won't return.

There are different degrees of intensity in the struggle for significance, to be sure! But to the woman feeling insecure, knowing someone else may feel worse than she does at the moment helps very little to alleviate the need for approval and acceptance.

Several years ago Dr. James Dobson described what it *feels* like for a woman to have low self-esteem:

> It is sitting alone in a house during the quiet afternoon hours, wondering why the phone doesn't ring . . . wondering why you have no "real" friends. It is longing for someone to talk to soul to soul, but knowing there is no such person worthy of your trust. It is feeling that "they wouldn't like me if they knew the real me." It is becoming terrified when speaking to a group of your peers, and feeling like a fool when you get home. It is wondering why other people have so much more talent and ability than you do. It is feeling incredibly ugly and sexually unattractive. It is admitting that you have become a failure as a wife and mother. It is disliking everything about yourself and wishing, constantly wishing, you could be someone else. It is feeling unloved and unlovable and lonely and sad. It is lying in bed after the family is asleep, pondering the vast emptiness inside and longing for unconditional love. It is intense self-pity.

It is reaching up in the darkness to remove a tear from the corner of your eye. It is depression![3]

Our deepest sense of significance always comes when a valued person conveys unequivocally that we are uniquely and distinctly important, personally acceptable, approved of, and profoundly wanted.

OUR LONGING FOR ACCEPTANCE

The need to feel special began in the Garden of Eden. God created man to have fellowship with Himself. Then God created Eve to have fellowship with Adam and to complement him. From the very beginning, relationships were meant to bring joy, completeness, acceptance, and significance to human beings. We were created for God's pleasure and companionship. He ordained that we should enjoy each other and that our significance would come from Him.

But Satan is a great deceiver! Not only did he destroy the perfect relationship Adam and Eve had with God, he also began strategically planting ungodly doubts in the hearts of every man and woman who has been born since that time.

The list of people who doubted how special they were reads like *Who's Who in Scripture.*

Moses: God's chosen leader of the Exodus despised his own humanity: "Who am I, that I should go to Pharaoh and bring the Israelites out of Egypt? . . . O Lord, I have never been eloquent, neither in the past nor since you have spoken to your servant. I am slow of speech and tongue. . . . O Lord, please send someone else to do it" (Exodus 3:11; 4:10,13).

Joshua: The Lord's inspiring challenge to Joshua gives us a glimpse of his insecurity: "Be strong and courageous. Do not be terrified; do not be discouraged, for the LORD your God will be with you wherever you go" (Joshua 1:9).

David: One day David sat before the Lord and thoughtfully said, "Who am I, O Sovereign LORD, and what is my family, that you have brought me this far? And as if this were not enough in your sight, O Sovereign LORD, you have also spoken about the future of the house of your servant. Is this your usual way of dealing with man . . . ?" (2 Samuel 7:18-19).

Elijah: God had just destroyed 450 prophets of Baal, but Jezebel entered the scene and . . . "Elijah was afraid and ran for his life. . . . He came to a broom tree, sat down under it and prayed that he might die. 'I have had enough, LORD, . . . Take my life; I am no better than my ancestors'" (1 Kings 19:3-4). Elijah's struggle for significance came after intense, exhausting ministry that left him physically weak and spiritually drained.

Jeremiah: Could anyone have felt less adequate than Jeremiah when God told him his main job as a prophet would involve numerous and demanding responsibilities? "Ah, Sovereign LORD . . . I do not know how to speak; I am only a child" (Jeremiah 1:6).

When we think realistically about the accomplishments of these great biblical leaders, it's easy to smile and wonder how in the world they *ever* doubted their significance—especially to God! But if I look at myself honestly, I understand. If the Enemy can make me feel unloved, insignificant, worthless, alone, inadequate, and friendless, I become incapable of being a secure Christian woman who has a positive impact on my family, my work, and my ministry.

THE GREAT MYSTERY

The dynamic, successful Bible leaders mentioned above struggled with the same dilemma you and I face every day. We consistently confuse *what we do* with *who we are*. Subliminally there is a feeling that if we could be smart enough, gifted enough, or successful enough (even in Christian work), then we would be significant in God's eyes. There is something inside us that longs to *earn* our place on God's "approval" list.

For years I worked myself to a frazzle trying to be special to God—always confusing *doing* with *being*. One day, in worn-out desperation, I shouted my sob to God, "Lord, I'm trying to be a five-talent person in a two-talent body, and I can't do it any more!" I was suffering under the delusion that if I would say yes to every ministry opportunity that came along, I would be more special to God and to other Christian people I longed to impress.

What Really Happens?

As I've stated earlier, we have an inborn expectation to feel special—to God and to other people. We were designed by God to enjoy perfect relationships in a perfect, pre-fallen world. When there is a discrepancy between our expectations and reality, disappointment sets in, causing a deep desire for change. This longing produces an initial emotion, an automatic response which screams out, "If I don't feel significant, life isn't worth living!" As we run those emotions through the grid of our convictions and values, a ruling passion takes over and drives us in one of two directions: one that pleases God or one that reflects our twisted thinking.

What Happened to Meg?

When we look back at Meg's story, we can see the problem as it develops.

Meg's Expectation: Meg had a deep and natural expectation that she would be special to her parents, that they would see her as a valued and important part of the family.

Meg's Disappointment: Her disappointment came over a period of years as she observed her parents' attention to her pretty sister and her only brother. The disappointment was reinforced as her dramatic abilities were not given the same value as her brother's athletic achievements.

Meg's Longing: Out of her deep disappointment, Meg's longing was born: a deep desire for approval, value, respect, and worth from the people most important to her—her mom and dad!

Meg's Emotion: Hurt hardly begins to describe what Meg felt as a result of her parents' rejection. She was crushed. The little girl in her agonized over having what she most longed for completely out of reach. Her hurt and shame gave way to a boiling anger and bitterness.

Meg's Decision: Running her painful emotions through a damaged values system, Meg made a decision. Life devoid of affirmation from the people she loved was too painful. She didn't dare explore her unfulfilled longings in light of God's truth and discover her security and significance in Him. She had to find another way to ease her current pain.

Meg's Drive/Passion: Meg was driven by a passion for relief from her pain—at all costs. And the cost nearly destroyed her life.

Meg's Action: Meg's ruling passion drove her to seek a sense of specialness and self-worth by excelling and then by rebelling. Her initial hurt propelled her to workaholic tendencies in an effort to *earn* her parents' approval. When that didn't work, she turned her back on her Christian upbringing and decided to practice destructive, rebellious behavior in a final attempt to gain their attention.

After her initial outburst of atypical, boisterous, and inappropriate behavior, she turned inward, withdrawing from people and burying herself in deep depression. She became pregnant by the first man who paid attention to her and married him too quickly. His violent physical abuse caused her physical as well as emotional pain, and her distorted values system reminded her that she was a "nothing" and probably deserved to be treated with disrespect.

Meg's negative, ungodly, ruling passion propelled her into a lifestyle of sadness, depression, hopelessness, and spiritual devastation. For Meg, the long healing process back to spiritual and emotional wholeness has begun, but there are scars that will last a lifetime.

WHERE DO WE FIT?

Most women have far less dramatic stories than Meg, but all of us can see a part of our innermost being in her situation. If we were raised by parents who held us tenderly, who verbally affirmed our great worth, who consistently "dreamed great dreams for our future" while actively helping us to pursue those dreams, we were fortunate indeed! We probably have a very positive picture of who God is and how valuable we are to Him, too. But if we had parents who failed to love us this well (and most of us did), we may have a hard time experiencing the love of our heavenly Father. Unfortunately, we tend to view God a great deal like we view our earthly parents.

I was sitting in an audience listening to a wardrobe consultant when she pointed out the importance of honesty. Her best advice was to take a few private moments at home to lock ourselves in our bathroom, strip down to the flesh, and stand in front of a full-length mirror and itemize our assets and liabilities. After we quit laughing, we all admitted that it was a great way to evaluate where we needed help—with exercise, diet, and camouflage!

Sometimes I wish we all could do that same exercise mentally and strip down to our bare motives, longings, passions, desires, and drives. Wouldn't it be interesting to weigh our activities on a scale that could automatically tell us whether we're living in an attempt to be special to God or to other people, or whether we have discovered the truth that *who we are* in His sight is more important than *what we do*?

What a helpful tool it would be for all of us who have struggled with low self-esteem to be able to have a device that would chronologically flash a videotape of our lives on a screen and point out the critical points in life where our disappointments produced longings for change. If we could only evaluate our emotional responses *before* deciding on a negative, destructive ruling passion, in many cases *years* of a difficult, depressing existence might be avoided.

WHERE CAN SIGNIFICANCE BE FOUND?

I have always enjoyed an intellectual challenge, and one of my favorite activities continues to be "creative verbal sparring" with people who have definite opinions about religion, politics, current issues, and impossible dreams. As a firstborn, obsessive-compulsive, driven, type-A personality, much of my *feeling* of worth has come from what I do, who I'm with, and how many items are crossed off my "To Do" list by the end of the day. I'm not proud of that.

The lesson I'm still learning is that *I am valuable to God.* No flash. No media blitz. No big-time drama. No need to impress Him with my accomplishments, my associates, my looks, or my wardrobe. The plain and simple truth is that He finds me special!

With my personality, my sense of worth is at great risk when I accomplish far less than what my daily list requires, or when my schedule is drastically affected by unexpected interruptions or prolonged projects. Feelings of failure swoop in like birds of prey, leaving me feeling worthless and insignificant.

My expectation of being a "model Christian woman" has been disappointed again! I immediately long for a change. At the deepest level my longing is to have my disappointments filled with the satisfaction of God Himself. But emotions grip me. If I can pause at this point and think rationally about *who He is* and *who I am to Him,* my ruling passion will not be crazy workaholism (trying to "earn" His approval) or severe withdrawal ("I've failed before, and I'm a failure again, so I might as well quit trying.").

The bottom line is that God Himself finds me significant—so special, in fact, that He's given me the five crucial elements that authors Gary Smalley and John Trent identify in *The Blessing*:

- Meaningful touch
  God touches my life everyday through His Word, His creation, and through other people. When a fellow believer puts an arm around me, sends a note of encouragement, or phones to say she's praying for me, I feel affirmed, special, and valued.
- A spoken message
  Repeatedly in Scripture we are given a spoken message of love and affirmation. The Lord says in Jeremiah 31:3, "I have loved you with an everlasting love; I have drawn you with loving-kindness."
- Attaching "high value" to the one being blessed

What greater value could we ask for than to be created in the image of our heavenly Father? (Genesis 1:27).

- Picturing a special future for the one being blessed
  Throughout the Bible, God reminds us of the unique, personally designed future He has already planned for us: "You have made known to me the path of life; you will fill me with joy in your presence, with eternal pleasures at your right hand" (Psalm 16:11).
- An active commitment to fulfill the blessing
  The day we realize *we are not alone* is a very important day! Paul assures us of God's continuing involvement in fulfilling His purpose through us when he writes, "Being confident of this, that he who began a good work in you will carry it on to completion until the day of Christ Jesus" (Philippians 1:6).[4]

POSTSCRIPT TO A NOBODY

In her book *God's Joyful Surprise,* Sue Monk Kidd beautifully states the depth of our longing:

> The deepest need of the human heart is to be loved. To be loved utterly and completely just as we are, no matter what. We respond to this need in a lot of different ways. Sometimes we try to be perfect in order to earn love. Or we repress our need until all that remains of it is a vague sense of restlessness and yearning. And meanwhile, inside that secret place which God fashioned for us to dwell with Him, we grow hungrier, emptier. The experience of God as a loving, encompassing reality in the midst of our days can be the most elusive one of our lives.[5]

Satan, the father of lies, the greatest deceiver of all time, knows that when our expectations of being special to someone are disappointed, we will long for change. If he can move quickly, we will be caught up in our emotions and make a bad decision based on ungodly values. If he succeeds, our ruling passion will drive us to work to earn approval, or to practice inappropriate behavior in an attempt to gain attention, or to withdraw.

But if we can evaluate our disappointments in time, we can choose a different course of action. By taking that deep longing for significance through the grid of our Christian convictions, our ruling passion will lead us to a decision that will glorify the God who created us.

> It is God who loved us first. His unceasing love sends Him after us. He is the seeking Lover, the one who has made us for Himself. From the very beginning we were created to be found and loved by Him. He has woven this secret into the very fibers of our soul, and when we seek Him with all the longing He has planted in our hearts, in the end, we simply discover Him seeking us, loving us—in all times and all places.[6]

Our deepest passion for significance is finally satisfied when we realize He is all we need and we are "somebody" to Him.

FOUR

I WANT TO DO SOMETHING WORTHWHILE
To Have Meaningful Work

*It is not what a man does that determines whether his
work is sacred or secular, it is why he does it.
The motive is everything. Let a man sanctify the
Lord God in his heart and he can thereafter do no
common act.*
A. W. TOZER

"**A**nd what do *you* do for a living?" The sophisticated woman
peered at me over her half-glasses and waited for a response.
I stammered and broke eye contact while floundering for an
image-building response.

For a brief moment I was speechless. Then, with a stutter,
I blurted out, "I-I-I'm in education, but we moved recently, so
I left my job as director of an Alternative Education Program
for Pregnant Teenagers, so I guess you'd say I'm a homemaker
right now. I used to individualize course work so pregnant
teens could stay in school during their pregnancies. Part of my
job involved coordinating the efforts of school social workers,
health care professionals, and the parents of the girls. It was
the most fulfilling work I've ever had."

My face flushed. I was embarrassed for having given such
a lengthy description of my *former* position. I had never realized how much my self-esteem was locked into my professional

status in the field of education. My husband had accepted a job that necessitated a move to another state, and for the first time in years I was without the significance connected with my former occupation. My security blanket was gone!

I held the firm belief that *what* a person did for a living had nothing to do with her worth, intelligence, or value. But here I was, feeling like a nobody who had to apologize for joining the ranks of the "domestic engineers" by describing the details of my former "real" job.

My internal feedback was somewhat muddied, but I knew my response was a desperate attempt to be viewed as an important person by a woman I didn't even know. That realization immediately made me feel like a spiritual failure. "*Good* Christian women shouldn't need a title, an engraved brass plate on their front door, or a briefcase in their hands to know they are significant," I told myself. "*So why am I playing this game?*"

ANALYZING THE REACTION

When we meet someone for the first time, the question comes within minutes: "What do you do?" We're quick to assess a person's worth by our evaluation of the importance of their work. That leads us to the source of the disappointments of millions of women—even Christian women.

We have an expectation that we will have meaningful work which will provide a sense of worth. That expectation is often unfulfilled when our dreams of higher education are cut short, or when a baby interrupts our career, or when motherhood is not granted the "professional" status it deserves, or when we are trapped in a job beneath our aptitude or level of training, or when good health is taken from us. Sometimes our disappointment comes with a gradual realization that day follows day and year follows year and we never seem to accomplish anything that seems important or significant.

As Christian women we have a deep longing to see God's purpose in our day-to-day activities. *We have a passion to know we are doing something worthwhile with our lives.*

THE SECULAR VALUES SYSTEM

In a recent poll conducted for Robert Half International, a New York-based firm, the findings indicated that "one out of four Americans is unhappy in his or her job. The reasons? Workers most often mentioned their need for greater recognition, more money, less stress, and a better boss."[1]

In another study, "90 percent of U.S. high school students and 88 percent of their parents maintain that the primary purpose for a college education is to secure a job when you get out of school, make money, and eventually take it easy."[2]

As we listen to those in the media and talk with people on an everyday basis, there appear to be two reasons why the average person in twentieth-century America works outside the home.

First, to earn enough money to pay the bills and then to use the excess to enjoy life and accumulate "things." There's a popular bumper sticker that voices this philosophy: He who dies with the most toys wins. Or maybe you've seen the television commercial with the camera zooming in on an attractive couple sipping cool drinks on a sunny beach. A voice beckons, "While your friends are freezing in Minnesota, experience the good life with us in the Caribbean!" Many people view work as a "necessary evil" that is simply a means of attaining personal pleasure.

Second, to define "who I am." Many people are driven to succeed in their work in order to feel good about themselves. We somehow feel that what we *do* should describe what we *are*. This false philosophy is the trap I found myself in after leaving a fulfilling job when my husband was transferred.

Both Christian and nonChristian women struggle with the need to do something worthwhile. The person who attains enough wealth to pay the bills for every consumer product she desires soon winds up with an empty spirit if nothing is invested in the lives of other people. Some of us are driven by insecurity to become workaholics, only to find we're exhausted, unhappy, and struggling with feelings of failure. Too often we run our emotions through a distorted secular values system.

How Does It Work?

Let me attempt to explain the process.

Our Expectation: As Christian women we have a passionate desire to have a mission in life that validates our worth.

Our Disappointment: When we lose a meaningful job or when we become overwhelmed with the routine and sometimes frantic commitments of day-to-day living, we feel defeated. We feel robbed of our true "mission." Recently a woman wrote to me, frankly reporting her frustrations.

> As a young pastor's wife, mother of an infant, church bulletin maker, the minister's secretary (I'm married to him), director of the Awana Youth Program, and lay counselor for anyone who calls my house at *any* hour, I become very drained. My life is so busy with urgent situations, programs, and people that I sometimes wonder if I'm really using my best gifts and if I'm living up to my fullest potential. Who am I and what am I really worth to God?

If our mission is something we want, and it has been taken away, we're disappointed. If, however, it's a mission that's been "thrust upon us," we may feel just as disappointed, wondering if the massive busyness is really accomplishing God's purpose.

Our Longing: Our disappointment leads to a desire for change. At the deepest level our desire is for a mission that fulfills God's agenda on earth. We long to know what our precise, customized task is that will validate our worth to Him and others.

Our Emotion: At this point the inner churning begins, and a variety of emotionally charged thoughts (and comments) emerge.

• "If I can't have that job, I'll never feel good about myself!"

• "I get so angry when I'm expected to do all this busywork; I never have time to do important things for God."

Our Decision: With a basic knowledge of Scripture, our logic should lead us to a well-informed decision. Intellectually we know that God created us, loves us intensely, and every activity in life has the potential of being used in an uncommon way for God's glory. As His ambassadors on this earth, we have a position of great significance as we faithfully live out our daily lives.

Our problem comes when we sift our emotions through the world's values system. As we mull over the familiar old question, "What do *you* do for a living?" and as we view the status of those around us who have accumulated wealth, power, and prestige, we sometimes reach an ungodly decision.

Our Drive/Passion: If our values are securely rooted in the Word of God, we'll be convinced of our overwhelming worth to God regardless of our title, position, or "measurable" value. If, however, our convictions have been twisted by the way the secular world views "important people," we are likely to have a ruling passion that will lead us to depression or workaholism.

Our Action: The ruling passion will determine our action. I was very disappointed when my husband accepted the position that robbed me of a significant job. There was a major emotional struggle as I reviewed my situation, and lots of discussion with Gene about our options. But ultimately, I knew my significance to God was not tied to my job with pregnant teens. With a values system based on His Word, I was able to have a ruling passion that could result in an honorable action. In my case it was moving with my husband to a new location and believing I would be just as valuable to God without the benefit of my former position. (There were also special, unexpected benefits for me in this move that I had not anticipated.)

WHAT IS "MEANINGFUL" WORK?

Experts refer to work as "purposeful activity" that is revealed in three biblical dimensions: *expression*—that which expresses our abilities; *provision*—that which provides for our needs; and *mission*—that which accomplishes God's agenda on this earth.

As a Christian woman, I have spent the last several years of my life working in both secular employment and full-time Christian ministry. I am fully convinced that for the Christian there is no difference between the secular and the sacred with regard to the energy expended and the potential spiritual fruitfulness in both situations.

Working with women in Bible study and conference ministry for the past ten years has allowed me to counsel with enough individuals to learn that *all* women struggle with their self-worth when it comes to discovering their gifts and finding meaningful work. Most of us can point to at least one other woman who *appears* to have the perfect life situation that we secretly wish belonged to us.

For both married and single women, there are fabulous advantages and horrendous disadvantages to every life situation we could secretly desire, yet our sense of significance is intricately connected to our position and work in this world.

In the home in which I was raised, a high premium was placed on listening to God and then doing His will. It was more important than fancy houses, luxury automobiles, impressive titles, or public acclaim.

During my junior high and high school years, my father made an indelible impression on me. After having run from God's call to the ministry for several years, Dad went back to Bible school and soon left the business world behind. With a wife and several children to support, it must have been a difficult decision. As I began my ninth-grade year, Dad took his first pastorate. Those were exciting days!

I watched Mom and Dad as they began to pour their lives into needy people. Mom's gift of hospitality and Dad's gift of evangelism worked like a hand in a glove to "love people into the Kingdom of God."

"BURNING BUSH MENTALITY"

Going through my high school years during this high point in my parents' ministry meant that I was constantly exposed to Christianity at its most dramatic level. By the time I left home for my university years, I longed with every fiber of my being to make a difference in my world for Jesus Christ. The feeling must have been a lot like what Ray Ortlund, pastor of Lake Avenue Congregational Church in Pasadena, California, expressed in one of his books:

> I had exclaimed in anguish many times in my life, "I refuse to be an ordinary Christian!"
> I had pounded the pulpit and said, "I refuse to be an ordinary pastor! I refuse to pastor an ordinary church!"
> Then I read a sentence from Thomas Kelly that set my heart on fire. He prayed, "Lord, make my life a miracle."
> Oh, God! That's it! You're the original Miracle, and I live in You. Why shouldn't I be able to show others how to be miracles?[3]

I didn't yet know what God's plan was for my life, but one thing was certain—I was looking for my "burning bush" and I longed to hear Him tell me (preferably through a megaphone or on a neon sign) what He wanted me to do. He had worked dramatically in my parent's lives, and I expected the same. My significance would come from Him!

Promptly, I selected Psalm 16:11 in the King James Version as my life verse: "Thou wilt shew me the path of life: in thy presence is fulness of joy; at thy right hand there are pleasures for evermore." I was actively looking for my unique, personalized, immediate, and specific directions for following God's plan for my life. I was ready to set the world on fire!

My Selfish Demand

In Old Testament times, God often did the unusual to get the attention of people He was calling for important tasks. This was a day and age when the Holy Spirit did not reside within the hearts of men and women who believed in Him. There was no written Word of God in existence yet.

One of the Old Testament accounts that has always thrilled me is Exodus 3:2-5,9-10:

There the angel of the LORD appeared to him in flames
of fire from within a bush. Moses saw that though the
bush was on fire it did not burn up. So Moses thought,
"I will go over and see this strange sight—why the bush
does not burn up."

God called to him from within the bush, "Moses!
Moses!"

And Moses said, "Here I am."

"Do not come any closer," God said. "Take off your
sandals, for the place where you are standing is holy
ground. . . . The cry of the Israelites has reached me,
and I have seen the way the Egyptians are oppressing
them. So now, go. I am sending you to Pharaoh to bring
my people the Israelites out of Egypt."

I know I'm not the only person who would like to hear
God's voice in such a direct manner. The drama of the bush
that could not be consumed by fire, and God's voice speaking
Moses' name from within has always made me long for an
emotionally charged calling for myself.

When I read this account in Scripture, I expect God to do
something *big, flashy*, and *personal* for me, too. I'm often looking for specific instructions for significant tasks, and when my
mind is thus engaged I sometimes miss God's most important
voice to me through His Word. It can become a subtle arro-
gance that cries, "Lord, if You don't show me Your will soon,
I'll know I'm not *really* important to You."

Such an attitude must grieve the heart of God. So often
He is quietly at work in powerful ways, revealing His will as
I continue being faithful in the daily affairs of life. Augustine
wrote, "You were guiding me as a helmsman steers a ship, but
the course You steered was beyond my understanding."[4]

The fact is, God's purpose for our lives is already spelled
out clearly in Ephesians 1:9,11-14:

He made known to us the mystery of his will according
to his good pleasure. . . . In him we were also chosen,
having been predestined according to the plan of him

who works out everything in conformity with the purpose of his will, in order that we . . . might be for the praise of his glory. Having believed, you were marked in him with a seal, the promised Holy Spirit, who is a deposit guaranteeing our inheritance until the redemption of those who are God's possession—to the praise of his glory.

Our main goal in life is to live for "the praise of His glory." He has made the mystery of His will known to us and blessed us with the indwelling Holy Spirit.

On top of all that, He has uniquely gifted us for service. Read Romans 12:4-8, 1 Corinthians 12:27-31, and Ephesians 4:11-13. As we study these passages, we discover that there is no gender differentiation related to gifts given in the Body of Christ. You and I are special to God, with significant gifts in the Body of Christ. Without our contribution the Body suffers.

I long to praise Him with the gifts, time, energy, and opportunities He has given to me during this lifetime. In his book *Desiring God,* John Piper stated,

God's pursuit of praise from us and our pursuit of pleasure in him are one and the same pursuit. God's quest to be glorified and our quest to be satisfied reach their goal in this one experience: our delight in God which overflows in praise. For God, praise is the sweet echo of his own excellence in the hearts of his people. For us, praise is the summit of satisfaction that comes from living in fellowship with God.[5]

For me, living in fellowship with God and praising Him with my life involves working for Him. Work was meant to be a fulfilling experience. In fact, work was created *before* the fall of man, as we can see from Genesis 2:15: "The LORD God took the man and put him in the Garden of Eden to work it and take care of it." God knew that you and I needed meaningful work to be fulfilled human beings.

For many Christian women, parenting is a great work God gives them for a season of their lives. Ellen Wilson Fielding was book editor of the *Wall Street Journal,* married at age twenty-eight, and some time later she gave birth to a son. She tells of the varied reactions of the people close to her when she announced she would be leaving her prestigious position to become an at-home mother. Her response? "I felt I was going to a greater thing when I left the *Wall Street Journal* to care for my son, because I was setting out to give more, more intensely, to a single human soul than I had been able to give for the millions of souls mildly affected by the book reviews I prepared for publication."[6]

Fielding's direction from the Lord may be different than His leading in your life or in my life; however, often the most fulfilling work we could have is the most obvious opportunity in our path today. Life is full of a panorama of opportunities to accomplish God's agenda on this earth. How sad it would be to miss the joy of today because we were looking for a more spectacular mission.

CHANGING TIMES—UNCHANGING GOD

In a recent article in *Christianity Today,* Ruth Tucker gives us statistics that shape the nation. What's really happening in our world today?

> In the course of just one generation a startling change has occurred in the role of mothers. In 1950, only 12 percent of married women with children under the age of six were employed outside the home; by 1987, that figure had grown to more than 50 percent, according to statistics published by the Population Reference Bureau.
>
> Perhaps the most compelling reason that mothers have entered the work force in recent years is the rise of single-parent households. By 1986, 10 million families in America—one in every six—were financially supported by a woman. This situation has been caused largely by the increased divorce rate and the escalation of teenage

pregnancies, which have forced women into full-time work to provide the bare necessities for themselves and their children.

Some experts predict that by 1995, 80 percent of women between the ages of 25 and 44 will be in the work force, and the majority of them will be mothers.[7]

For working women, especially single working moms, time is very scarce. It's easy to feel that the day-to-day demands of life, work, and parenting keep us from embracing our real purpose. The Enemy sees our vulnerability and is quick to bring disappointments to mind. It's easy to long for a simpler life and for a greater opportunity to be involved in a more "meaningful" task. We can keep our emotions from dragging us into a twisted ruling passion by understanding that the job God has allowed us to have is the perfect opportunity to experience life under the lordship of Christ. Being obedient to Him in *today's* task is just as holy a calling as reaching our full potential in the future.

DEVELOPING A BIBLICAL VALUES SYSTEM

It's clear that each of us is uniquely gifted for specific Christian service, whether we use our gifts in the secular or Christian arena. But where should we start when we have major questions about how God wants to use us? I believe there are at least five things we can do to discover the answers to those questions and make sure we are investing our lives in the things that are important to God.

Spend Time in Solitude Every Day.

There's an old proverb that says, "Listen, or thy tongue will make thee deaf." My life can easily consist of waking up to the radio, the coffee pot, the shower, the daily stresses, the television, phone calls, and meal preparations, and if I have not pre-scheduled and *seized* a time to be alone with the Lord, there is none.

Sometimes my days are filled with the voices of other

people—in person as well as through the media. I wonder if God sometimes tries to say, "Carol, I have something I'd like to tell you if I could get through the commotion so you could hear Me."

When you are alone with Him, make a special study of the God-given gifts mentioned in Scripture. (The passages were mentioned earlier in this chapter.) Ask your pastor or another trusted Christian friend to recommend a good book on discovering your gifts. As you study, pray, "Lord, what am I uniquely gifted to do in Your Kingdom? How can You best be glorified in me?"

Discover How You're Wired.
For instance, you may have the specific spiritual gift of "helps" or "showing mercy," but you are really *wired* for a career in nursing. Other people may walk into a hospital, breathe the medicinal aroma, and feel ill themselves. You walk down the corridor of a health care facility and your natural instinct is to *do something* for one of the patients.

You may attend a conference and immediately notice the lack of organization surrounding the scheduling, crowd control, and registration process. Your immediate reaction is to mentally lay out the way things *should have been done* to avoid confusion and problems. You have a God-given gift of "administration," and you are goal-oriented, efficient, and decisive. When you chair a committee, organize the church Christmas program, or function as a chief executive officer, everything runs smoothly and you feel good about it.

I'm *wired* for exhortation. When I'm with a group of believers and someone is struggling in a new position, I'm usually first to "come alongside" as a cheerleader and encourager. I've been training Christians in communication skills in my "Speak Up With Confidence" seminars for the last few years, and almost nothing brings me more joy than seeing someone with potential for sharing their faith or teaching the Word of God gain the confidence to speak up for Him!

I love to "drive home" specific truths from Scripture in such a way that people are motivated and deeply encouraged in their walk with God. My whole being wants to shout, "Hang in there! You can make it! Don't give up! You've just begun! I'm on your side!"

Study Your Motivational Pattern.
In their book *Finding a Job You Can Love,* authors Ralph Mattson and Arthur Miller tell us:

> The motivational pattern is evidence that God has designed us not as haphazard collections of possibilities, but as people with highly detailed gifts that differ from one individual to another. . . . We have a mode of action, a certain way of operating that is unique to us and that calls us to be what we were made to be, not what others want us to be.[8]

The authors carefully explain a series of elements that help us determine our unique design. To paraphrase:

- What is your *central motivational* thrust? What is the outcome you are motivated to achieve?
- What are the *abilities* you are motivated to use?
- What is the *subject matter* with which you love to work?
- What are the *circumstances* within which you enjoy functioning?
- How do you best *relate to and operate with* people?[9]

I believe that God has gifted each of us in such a way that there are moments, while we are exercising our gift, that we have an inexplicable urge to shout, "Eureka!" That word is an interjection that indicates, "I found it!" It's a proclamation of surprise or pleasure upon finding that for which we've been looking.

Some time ago I was seated in a theater watching an exceptional film titled *Chariots of Fire*. This was the story of Eric Liddell, who later became a missionary to China, until his death in the 1940s. As an Olympic athlete Eric was in conflict regarding his giftedness and his personal convictions. He suddenly blurted out, "God made me so I run fast, and when I run I *feel* His pleasure."

I got a "catch" in my throat as he spoke. That's exactly how I feel when I teach people the Word of God and encourage them to be their best for the King of kings. God made me so I speak well. He designed me to be an encourager of other people, and when I use that gift I'm experiencing the joy of living in the smile of God's approval. Every believer can experience this. Each can discover her unique gift and present it to the Lord as a living sacrifice, for "the praise of His glory."

Exercise Your Spiritual Muscle.
In prayer, dedicate yourself, your known gifts, your knowledge (however limited), and your *potential* to the Lord. Expose yourself to various tasks. Take advantage of opportunities to develop your gifts. Be actively pursuing God's highest calling for you!

Tim Hansel's writing always makes me smile. When I'm through chuckling, I'm convicted. In a recent book *Holy Sweat* (yes, that really *is* the title!), he says,

> Can we astonish God? We may not think we have the qualifications to, but think of Moses, and Peter, and Mary Magdalene and a host of the other biblical characters. None of them was "qualified." Doesn't that give us hope and encouragement that God can use any of us? All of us? God is saying to us, "Don't just exist. Don't just meet my bottom line. Don't just go through the motions, acting holy, sleepwalking through life."
>
> Thankfully, he keeps offering the adventure to us. He still says, "Astonish me! Let the herd graze where they may, but you be different. Discover my power in you. Live your theology as biography."[10]

Listen to the Responses of Others.
There are two extremes that sadden my heart as I travel in ministry and hear the responses of women with regard to

using God's gifts. One is the response of the woman who does not dare to believe God will do great things when He has opened every door for service, but instead continues to do nothing while saying, "Me? I couldn't do *that!*" The other is the one who lives in a fantasy world of constantly wishing to have gifts that seem more glamorous than the obvious gifts she possesses.

How do you know for sure that you have a gift? Consider the discernment of the people around you. What they say will give you clues. If you've wondered if you have a gift for teaching, try it. If people approach you afterward and say, "God really ministered to me through you today" or "I've never heard the gospel presented in such a clear and practical way before," that's a great affirmation that you have a gift for teaching.

On the other hand, if people fall asleep while you're talking and no one gives you the feedback that your message was a help to them, consider that God may want you to do more homework and try again or that perhaps your main gift is in an entirely different area. How wonderful it is to find out!

The story is told of a young boy who was auditioning for a part in the school play. His mother knew that he'd set his heart on receiving a part, though she was afraid he would not be chosen. On the day the parts were awarded, she drove to the school to pick him up. He rushed up to her, eyes shining with pride and excitement as he exclaimed, "Mom! Mom! I've been chosen to clap and cheer!"

Our importance to the Body of Christ is discussed in 1 Corinthians 12:14-31: "Now the body is not made up of one part but of many. . . . God has arranged the parts in the body, every one of them, just as he wanted them to be. . . . Those parts of the body that seem to be weaker are indispensable. . . . Now you are the body of Christ, and each one of you is a part of it."

A PERSONAL CHALLENGE

I love to believe that God will do the impossible in the lives of ordinary people. Perhaps Bruce Larson said it best:

I believe God is waiting and willing to reveal things that will radically change the lives of people. I believe He is eternally waiting and eager to call forth something from you that has never been said or thought of since the beginning of time. You may be the one in your own field or area of interest to find that all the good things haven't been said or done or even thought of.[11]

Those thoughts stimulate and motivate me. But sometimes statements like that make me feel that if I don't come up with an idea, ministry, or opportunity that is somehow "exceptional," I'm not worth as much as the "brilliant" Christians.

When Elisabeth Elliot was preparing to write *A Slow and Certain Light,* she read through the whole Bible to discover how God guided people. She states,

> I found that in the overwhelming majority of cases
> it was not through what we'd call "supernatural"
> means—voices, visions, angels, or miracles—but by
> natural means in the course of everyday circumstances
> when a man was simply doing what he was supposed
> to be doing (taking care of sheep or fighting a battle or
> mending fishnets).[12]

That's encouraging to me because most of my days are ordinary. I've wasted a lot of time jumping from here to there trying to find "God's perfect will" when He's already placed me in an obvious place to serve Him today. We are exhorted in Ecclesiastes 9:10: "Whatever your hand finds to do, do it with all your might." I long to recognize God's voice and to do His will. And I can—today—*if I choose to see all ground as holy ground.*

PART THREE

THE PASSION
FOR SECURITY

FIVE

WHY ME? WHY THIS? WHY NOW?
To Accept Trials Gracefully

*True atheists do not, I presume, feel disappointed in
God. They expect nothing and receive nothing. But
those who commit their lives to God, no matter what,
instinctively expect something in return. Are those
expectations wrong?*
PHILIP YANCEY
Disappointment with God

The cover of the book intrigued me. A sticker on the front
offered a money-back guarantee. *Clever marketing idea,* I
thought. The book was the kind you hold with the title carefully concealed, so other people won't glance at your reading
material and automatically assume you have the problem
stated in the title. But I *did* have the problem, and I *had* to
buy that book! *Disappointment with God.*

I leafed through the first few pages and read Philip
Yancey's questions: *"Is God unfair?* Why doesn't he consistently punish evil people and reward good people? Why do awful
things happen to people good and bad, with no discernible pattern?" The author's questions continued: *"Is God silent? Is God
hidden?"*[1]

My mind was racing. I hated those questions! It seemed
blasphemous to think that God might be unfair, and it seemed
heretical to admit that thought to someone else. As a preacher's

kid, I'd memorized all the right answers. Romans 8:28 (KJV) was the "proper" response for all unexplainable grief: "And we know that all things work together for good to them that love God." I even had the manuscript of a talk I gave on suffering. It has three points—solid biblical points—that provided pat answers for the pain and hurts in the world. I hated that talk.

The day after I bought *Disappointment,* I declared a "day off" for myself. Dressed in jeans, I hurried through household chores so I could begin my reading. Within minutes I hated that book, too. Yancey asked questions without giving answers, and my personality type *demands* answers. I always buy "how-to" books that give ten solutions to a problem, with appropriate Scripture references listed with the correct answers—the kind of books Christian radio programs offer as premiums for gifts to their ministries. My basic philosophy has always been, "If you have a crisis, find out what caused it and fix it! If you look hard enough, pray intensely enough, and work long enough, you will discover the reason for your problem and there will be an obvious solution." Wrong!

DISAPPOINTMENT WITH GOD?

Draping my legs over an arm of my most comfortable chair, I "settled in." The feather cushion accepted the strange contours of my improper posture and formed a comfortable theater seat for the mental cinema that was about to begin. The deeply felt vignette would be from my life—a disappointment that I blamed God for (subliminally, of course, because I had never been able to admit that I was angry at Him).

My Expectation: Our son, J. P., was five years old, and Gene and I were thinking seriously about having another baby. We were comfortable in our spacious suburban home and felt God had blessed us with the love and resources to share with another child. When I worked in the church nursery, my mother heart beat faster as I held the babies close to my breast and dreamed about the possibility of another little one of my own.

To our surprise, the miracle of conception occurred sooner than we had anticipated. We weren't the youngest parents-to-be in our circle of friends, so we knew our "little secret" would be quite a surprise. We decided to wait a while to announce the good news. Sitting in church one Sunday morning, Gene put his arm around me and we took turns passing amused glances, first at my expanding waistline, then at each other. It wouldn't be long before the "secret" would announce itself if we didn't say something soon! Anticipation built with every passing day.

My Disappointment: One day as always, I was running at breakneck speed—kindergarten car pool for J. P., Bible Study Fellowship classes to teach, household responsibilities to tend to, correspondence to answer, and speeches to prepare. I had experienced some cramping during the early weeks of pregnancy and tried to slow my pace a bit. "It's normal," I told myself. "It's been so long since my last pregnancy. I just don't remember all these uncomfortable aches and pains that come with an expanding uterus." In spite of my rationalization, I had a nagging thought that the cramps were *not* normal.

The next day I left home early for a speaking engagement on the Canadian side of the border. Waiting to go through customs, I again felt painful abdominal tightening. Two hours into the trip, the cramps felt more like vise grips. Something was wrong. "Lord," I prayed, "please take care of this baby. I don't know what to do."

I was alone in a rural area in a foreign country, headed for a town with no hospital. The practical side of me took over and I gave myself a pep talk. "You've been having cramps regularly; this is no cause for alarm. You can stand this pain and make it through this speaking engagement. Over two hundred people are expecting you momentarily, and you can't let them down."

Arriving at my destination, I found myself in a community center and went immediately to the restroom. Graffiti covered the walls and filthy debris was scattered here and there on the floor. The smell indicated a desperate need for a plumber (or at least a custodian). My brief walk from the car was accompanied by severe abdominal pains, and sitting in that vulgar stall, I knew I was losing my baby. Within five minutes it was over. I was no longer pregnant.

The instant waves of depression were much worse than the physical discomfort, but I buried my emotions and went in to speak to those women.

My Longing: The meeting had already begun. After the introduction, I walked to the lectern. There, three rows back, directly in front of me, sat a woman with her darling infant in her arms. For an instant I didn't remember why I was there. She had a baby and I wanted one. The woman was holding what my heart longed for. I wanted my baby back in my womb, not flushed down a filthy toilet in a run-down community building!

My Emotion: I wanted to scream. It was so unfair. *God was so unfair!* Emotions pulsed through my heart and my breathing was irregular. My wild thoughts were directed heavenward. "Why? Why did You allow this to happen? I'm traveling alone. I am a good mother. I wanted that baby. Here I am serving You, working for You, investing my time in 'eternal stuff,' and You—God of the universe, Worker of miracles, mighty Healer—allowed me to lose this baby in that perverse, stinking washroom! Then, like rubbing salt in my wound, You allow that breast-feeding mother to sit in the third row! Yes, You are unfair!"

My Decision: It was time to begin. The pause before my opening remarks had already been too long. My internal furor, totally directed toward God, seemed foreign. With precise timing, guilt suddenly swept through me, temporarily knocking anger aside. My past years of Christian training provided a values system that I didn't instantly recognize as flawed. I told myself, "Mature Christians know God is in control during every crisis, even though they can't *see* Him at work. Forget your pain and do the right thing—give the speech and try not to look at the baby in the third row."

My Drive/Passion: If my values had been properly established on biblical truth, if I had been convinced of my security in Him as my Abba Father (my own dear Daddy), my ruling passion could have been acceptance of my pain and hurt, including the accompanying grief. Instead, my ruling passion was denial.

My Action: That day I carried on with my responsibilities like a programmed Christian robot. The speech I gave to that group was presented as if someone plugged a videotape into a VCR. It had predictable content and an evangelistic ending. I didn't admit my personal devastation to anyone in the group. On the way home I allowed myself the brief luxury of sobbing without embarrassment. My baby was gone! Then, almost as if on cue, I began my action of denial (which I truly believed was godly).

I minimized the physical pain and exhaustion I was feeling from the miscarriage. I pushed down the deep emotional agony of the loss and made light of the whole event with the handful of friends who knew about the pregnancy. By internally denying myself "mourning time" and instantly carrying on with major responsibilities, I was sure God would be more pleased with me.

THE PASSION FOR SECURITY

We have an insatiable desire for security! When we're secure, we feel safe and removed from danger. We experience freedom from doubt. True security makes us anxiety-free instead of worry-filled. There are three major places where we look for security, and when our expectations are unfulfilled in those areas we experience disappointment.

Possessions
As Christian women we know *real* security does not lie in what we possess, but often we're more attached to "things" than we might be able to admit. Several farmers in our area have been in deep financial difficulty due to the recent drought and low market prices of their commodities. One day my friend said, "Carol, when I became a farmer's wife I never considered that there would be a day I'd have to give up my home. We are going

bankrupt. I've been very upset, but my emotions went through the roof the day we had to sell my grandmother's china and silverware in an auction in order to liquidate our assets. Those items were heirlooms that would have been passed on to my children. I feel so guilty for crying about such a little thing. Before that auction I never knew how attached I was to 'things.' We are hard workers in our early forties, and every possession we have ever worked for has been taken from us. Surely God could have spared Grandma's china. *Why* is this happening to us? Sometimes it feels like a cruel joke." *Disappointment!*

Circumstances

It's easy to forget how often our security is tied to favorable circumstances. When events in our lives flow smoothly, life seems good. But when dramatic circumstances change the course of our lives, it's another story. A teenaged son is hit by a drunk driver and left with paralysis; a baby is born with Down's syndrome; a daughter gets hooked on drugs; a friend is raped and later discovers she is pregnant; a good job is lost; unexpected health problems occur. Suddenly, often without warning, we struggle with deep insecurities. *Disappointment!*

People

Relationships are the cause of our deepest joys and our most complex trials. It probably shouldn't surprise us. God created us for companionship. He created Eve to be the completer of Adam, and from the very beginning of the human race we have passionately longed for (and secretly expected) the security that comes from positive relationships with other people.

We feel like our heart is breaking in two when a husband leaves us, or our reputation is ruined by a co-worker, or our best friend turns on us. The experiences of birth and death can also be traumatic "shakers-of-security." In most cases, the deeper our experience of intimacy with another person, the greater the chance for hurt as a result of a misunderstanding, personal attack, or withdrawal. As Reuben Welch wrote several years ago, "We really do *need* each other!" And when our personal relationships are threatened, our security blanket is torn out of our hands. *Disappointment!*

Few things cause us the kind of surging emotion that a loss of security does, whether that comes through unexplainable trials or life's major change points. In the two chapters of this section there is some overlap, because usually a trial involves a change of some sort, and conversely, many changes are often trials. In this chapter, we're analyzing things and events that cause upsets in our lives, and in the next chapter we'll focus on different types of changes and how they affect our relationships. We're complex human beings, and trials and change-points usually interact with each other, even when we don't consciously realize it.

DIFFICULT QUESTIONS

It's hard to believe in the goodness of God when personal disaster strikes. Every day tragedies occur all around us. Our hearts want to scream, "Why, Lord? Where are You, God, when these horrible things happen? Do You care?"

One of our deep emotions of the heart is anger—even anger directed toward God—when we go through life's trials. There's something in us that fights back and cries out, "It's not fair! I don't deserve this! Why is this happening to me? Obviously God doesn't love me!" Then, as Christians, we feel guilty for having those thoughts.

THE GUILT SYNDROME

I have so much experience with guilt that I could start a franchise. I can see the neon sign now: "GUILT, INC., Founder and Director, Carol Kent. (Franchises available in your city with no money down)." The promotional material could advertise my credentials:

> Carol automatically feels guilty about everything she should have done or could have done better. She's a born people-pleaser. If you are unhappy with her performance, she knows she's wrong, not you. She feels

insecure if anyone in her sphere of influence sees her
as spiritually weak, and she feels responsible to automatically reflect the truth she teaches regarding biblical
principles. She feels especially guilty for occasionally
doubting God and for having negative thoughts about
His fairness. If her feelings of insecurity might be a
bad example to someone else, she will fake what her
Christian programming says is the proper response.
Her programming has been so complete that it's often
an automatic response that takes no thought at all. Frequently she feels like it's the "spiritual" thing to do.

Many of us who are active members of this exclusive
"guilt-trip" club have developed a flawed values system. Some
of the myths we have come to believe are the following:

- I must be a perfect Christian.
- Everyone should love me and approve of me.
- If I am a good Christian, life should be fair.
- It's a sin to feel depressed.
- If I am living in fellowship with God, I should never
  feel anger toward Him or other people.
- It's my job to meet everyone's needs.
- If I feel worried, I'm a bad Christian.
- If God loved me, bad things would not happen to
  me.
- God will bless me with health and happiness if I work
  hard for Him.
- When there is so much *real* tragedy in the world, it's
  wrong for me to feel grief over little things.

As the firstborn of six children, leadership was a "natural"
for me. Coming to know Christ at a young age and being raised
in the church gave me a wonderful background in biblical
truths and key Scriptures (which I memorized in the youth
training program). It wasn't until I evaluated my response following the loss of my baby that I began to admit how distorted
my values system had become.

I had expected a healthy baby that would fill our lives with more joy than we could imagine. Disappointment was keen on the day of the miscarriage. The dirty community center and the newborn in the audience intensified my great disappointment with God. I longed to pretend my loss was a dream and to wake to find that my miracle-working God had restored my pregnancy. Everything in my background taught me that God was fair. He was just. I knew nothing could touch me without His permission. Somehow that thought made me feel the miscarriage was His fault. As my decision-making process ran through my values system, which was a combination of truth and the myths I've just listed, my ruling passion became denial. With my twisted thinking pattern, my denial wound up driving me to several actions.

First, I didn't admit that I was physically weak and emotionally and spiritually devastated by the miscarriage.

Second, I lied to people by acting as if the loss was "no big deal . . . the baby was only in the embryo stage anyway . . . it wasn't like a stillbirth." (The lie wasn't consciously spoken; it was part of the conditioned response I thought a good Christian should give.)

Third, I experienced a "slow simmer" that gradually became a bubbling caldron of anger toward God for taking my baby and adding to my pain with so many negative happenings on the day of the miscarriage. The initial anger would not have become sin if I'd had a God-honoring ruling passion (to be totally transparent and honest with Him, committed to working *through* my feelings rather than allowing my anger to grow by pretending it wasn't there).

Fourth, over the next few years, creeping bitterness established a major root system within me. Occasionally someone would say, "I see you have only one child; I assume you're so busy in your career you really don't have time for the responsibility of another baby." (I felt like I'd been stabbed with a knife.)

One day a woman visited in my home and said, "I'd have nice furniture, too, if I'd chosen to have only one child and had gone to work." (Her unspoken accusation regarding my "materialistic" reason for being the mother of one made my blood boil!)

The crowning comment came when I was writing the manuscript for my first book. Two publishers were interested in the project, and at one point during the book proposal stage an editor phoned me and said, "In our editorial staff meeting today someone commented on the fact that you and your husband have only one child. As a Christian publishing house, we really believe in the family, and we're wondering *why* you decided to have a single child." Even though the question was asked politely, I felt misunderstood and violated. It was not their business! I again was being unjustly, though subtly, judged as a selfish person over one of the deepest hurts of my life. With emotions churning, I managed to give an "appropriate Christian response," but I signed a contract with the other publisher. (That one incident was not the only reason, but it *was* a contributing factor.)

If my values system had been based on true Christian principles, it would have included permission to experience deep grief; it would have freed me to acknowledge my physical condition the day I lost the baby. The Christian women's luncheon would not have been ruined if I had been unable to speak—even at the last minute. My values system should have included a clause that read: "She does not have to be a superwoman when life falls apart. She can cry when she hurts, and God will still love her if she acknowledges 'negative' emotions." With a ruling passion of denial, I didn't accept responsibility for sinful bitterness that affected my relationships with other people and with God over a period of years.

THE GUILT INTENSIFIES

I feel insecure when I'm not in control. That's a scary thing to admit. My disappointment with God does not come only in the major trials of life; it comes with the small stuff. One bitterly cold Saturday night last February, I was driving home from a conference. In pitch darkness on a very busy highway, my car suddenly lost all of its electrical power—no lights, no heat, no power steering!

Two hours later my hands were numb with cold, a mechanic I didn't know had total authority over my car (and my pocketbook), and I was told that it would be at least twenty-four hours before the "missing belt" on my vehicle could be replaced. Sitting in a motel in a strange city, I knew I would miss a scheduled meeting the next day and I would be liable for whatever the mechanic decided to charge. I felt like a victim, and I was angry at God.

Did God care about my tremendous frustration and my loss of time, money, and emotional energy? My disappointment brought a longing for change (a car that ran well, accompanied by no interruptions or financial distress). After expressing my negative emotions, first to the desk clerk and then to God, I felt guilty! Another myth came rushing in: *When there is so much real tragedy in the world, it's wrong for me to feel grief over little things.* Wrong again!

KILLING THE MYTHS AND BUILDING SOUND VALUES

I'm writing this book for people like me who want to learn the secret of handling disappointments in the right way, so the passions that rule us will be powerful forces for good rather than evil. If we are living by an internal list of myths that we believe are "spiritual," when indeed they are not, we will wind up with twisted, misguided ruling passions.

After responsibly facing the denial of the pain of my miscarriage, it was like someone lifted a veil off my understanding. Finally I could point to one incident after another in my life where I had sacrificed an honorable or a holy passion because I was living under a flawed values system. I reviewed my list of myths again:

- I must be a perfect Christian.
- Everyone should love me and approve of me.
- If I am a good Christian, life should be fair.
- It's a sin to feel depressed.

- If I am living in fellowship with God, I should never feel anger toward Him or other people.
- It's my job to meet everyone's needs.
- If I feel worried, I'm a bad Christian.
- If God loved me, bad things would not happen to me.
- God will bless me with health and happiness if I work hard for Him.
- When there is so much *real* tragedy in the world, it's wrong for me to feel grief over little things.

It was painful to admit that these "convictions" were not based on truth. I had based so many of my responses to trials in my life on flawed thinking, and my ruling passions resulted in actions that did not please God. Dr. Chris Thurman, psychologist at the Minirth-Meier Clinic in Dallas, Texas, says,

> Most of our unhappiness and emotional struggles are caused by the lies we tell ourselves. . . . Until we identify our lies and replace them with the truth, emotional well-being is impossible. . . . Lies are beliefs, attitudes, or expectations that don't fit reality. And we don't have to go out looking for them. They come to us. We learn our lies from a variety of sources—our parents, our friends, the culture we live in, even the church we attend. . . . Some of the lies we tell ourselves we know to be lies . . . some we believe have actually become the "truth" because we have practiced them for so long. These are the most dangerous lies of all because we rarely, if ever, dispute them. We don't dispute what we believe to be true.[2]

Replacing our myths with truth develops convictions that result in godly ruling passions. Instead of experiencing guilt for feeling and expressing our negative emotions and thus denying our pain, we can admit the struggle involved in the Christian life. It is not a sin to struggle. The Apostle Peter said, "Dear friends, do not be surprised at the painful trial you are suffering, as though something strange were happening to you" (1 Peter 4:12).

Bible teacher and conference speaker Dr. Stephen Olford once had a college student approach him with a question. The young man had his notebook and pen in hand and asked, "Tell me, what are the keys to Christian leadership?"

I'm sure this fellow was all set to write down ten easy steps to Christian maturity. Dr. Olford began, "The keys to Christian leadership are *bent knees, wet eyes,* and *a broken heart.*"3 Psalm 51:17 says, "The sacrifices of God are a broken spirit; a broken and contrite heart."

I sometimes forget that God designed me to live in a perfect world, but because of sin I live in a "groaning" world—filled with imperfect people, flawed values, disease, crime, war, unexplainable circumstances, and irritating Christians. My security is threatened when people let me down and when I let myself down again and again! If I believe my "myths," my ruling passions will be twisted.

Job reminds us that life is unfair and that being faithful to God does not mean our lives will automatically be filled with good health and happiness. Job's family died, his possessions were taken away, all circumstances that could turn on him did, his best friends thought he was a fool, and his wife told him to "curse God and die!"

In the middle of Job's trials, we feel his emotional response to his disappointments: "I cry out to you, O God, but you do not answer. . . . When I hoped for good, evil came; when I looked for light, then came darkness. The churning inside me never stops; days of suffering confront me" (Job 30:20,26-27). Job did not deny his pain; he trusted God through his anguish and expressed his hurt with imagery and deep emotion.

Healthy values allow us to recognize a disappointment, understand the longing it produces, *feel and express the pain of the emotional rush,* and run the decision-making process through truth—not myth—in order to choose a ruling passion that will glorify God as it becomes an action. David said in Psalm 56:8, "Record my lament; list my tears on your scroll—are they not in your record?" I wonder why, for most of my Christian life, I've buried my sorrow, denied my pain, and tried to be "a big girl for Jesus." *Faulty values!*

A week after speaking for a retreat, a letter arrived from one of the participants. She had never attended a Christian women's conference before and said she only came with her friend, Connie, because she wanted some time away and "the price was right." She wrote,

Dear Carol,
. . . after the first meeting, Connie and I knew we were meant to be there. We talked late on Friday night and all Saturday afternoon and I finally shared something I had determined I would never tell another soul. Even after the tears and comforting from Connie I could not pray—all I could feel was tremendous anger—and then the question—why? I was only eight years old. I didn't deserve it, and yet I have felt such tremendous guilt all these years!

When you started speaking and told about the sixteen-year-old who had trusted a man for a ride and how he raped her, my tears started again as my own memories of the past flashed before me.

When you asked if we knew that "bad things happen to good Christian people," the walls completely crumbled, and by the end of your talk I knew why I could not communicate with the Lord. I had completely closed communication with Him because I was so furious! I could not believe that He would have let that awful thing happen to me if He truly loved me. I had built my whole Christian life on a false set of ideals, forgetting that we live in a world that is fallen and full of hurts.

Feeding my emotions into faulty convictions, I believed that God was unfair, cruel, and hidden. My ruling passion, although I didn't consciously recognize it, was anger that was acted out by withdrawing from God and Christianity and building a wall between me and any human being who might hurt me. I'm just coming to grips with the fact that God does love me very much.

You encouraged me when you said that God could take *any negative* in our lives and turn it into a *positive*.

I'm thirty-nine years old and this is the first time I have genuinely experienced God's love, accepted what happened in my life, and expressed and released my anger. I have a long way to go, but this weekend was a new beginning for me.

CHANGING OUR THINKING TAKES TIME

I'm still reprogramming my mind with truth. I try to study biblical passages that replace my "myths" with statements that are based on fact. Insensitive comments about my "only" child don't hurt as much as they used to—but I can now admit that they *do* hurt! For me, that's a big step toward a more healthy values system. God doesn't expect me to be superhuman.

Memorizing Scripture has been a big help, but it's harder to memorize than it used to be and it's tough to climb out of old ruts, even if they're uncomfortable. Being honest about my emotions when I'm disappointed with God is still my most difficult hurdle, but I'm making progress. Philip Yancey's insights are a good reminder:

> The Spirit will not remove all disappointment with God. The very titles given to the Spirit—Intercessor, Helper, Counselor, Comforter—imply there will be problems. But the Spirit is also "a deposit, guaranteeing what is to come," Paul said, drawing on an earthly metaphor from the financial world. The Spirit reminds us that such disappointments are temporary, a prelude to an eternal life with God. God deemed it necessary to restore the spiritual link *before* re-creating heaven and earth.[4]

Right now life is hard and life is unfair. Larry Crabb reminds us that, while we live in this fallen world, we will groan, or pretend we don't![5] But my hope is firm and I have great security that there's a better day coming!

SIX

LORD, MAKE ME FLEXIBLE!
To Adapt to Change Joyfully

*If your security is based on something that can be
taken away from you—you will constantly be on a
false edge of security.*
TIM HANSEL

My heart sank as I opened a letter and read this note from
my friend Linda:

> Carol, my entire life has changed in a matter of a few
> weeks. My mother has been diagnosed with Alzheimer's
> disease and can no longer care for herself. She has
> moved into our home and totally disrupted my whole
> world. I was so looking forward to being with you for the
> "Speak Up With Confidence" seminar, but I'll need to
> cancel my registration and ask for your prayer. . . . I'm
> discovering that my mother has become my child and
> I have become her parent. On some days I handle the
> situation with dignity; at other times I scream and hit
> the walls.
>   My husband has informed me that he cannot cope
> with my mother by himself, even for a short time. He is

angry with the way she is interfering with every aspect
of our lives. We are fighting constantly and no longer
have any privacy.

This has been the most difficult change point in my
life. I love my mother deeply, but at times I can't stand
to be in the same room with her. She asks the same
questions repeatedly and there are days when I think
I'm going crazy. We can't afford full-time nursing care
for her, and the future looks hopeless.

A month earlier Linda had mailed her registration with
the attached note: "I've been waiting for this seminar for three
years—and I can hardly wait to be there! God continues to
open doors for me to speak, and I need more training. I'm
praying for you." Then suddenly, without warning, her whole
life was turned upside down by the health crisis of her mother.
All of her personal plans had to be put on hold.

One of my deep longings is to be strong enough as a Christian woman to adapt to change joyfully, no matter what! For
years I've quoted from such scriptures as, "but those who
hope in the LORD will renew their strength. They will soar
on wings like eagles; they will run and not grow weary, they
will walk and not be faint" (Isaiah 40:31). But I wonder if
I'd be "soaring like an eagle" if Linda's situation were mine.
I doubt it.

UNDERSTANDING CHANGE

I think of change as "anything that rocks my boat." And change
has great potential for threatening our sense of security. Some
changes are of major importance and determine how the next
several years of our lives will be lived. Other changes are much
less life-altering. Occasionally changes bring excitement, but
even when they're positive there's always some degree of stress
involved.

The experts tell us that traumas, transitions, and changes
occur throughout our lives and can usually be divided into the
following three groups.

Anticipated Changes

This category involves major life events that many of us expect to be part of our lives, such as entering the work force or getting married or having a child.

Unexpected Changes

These changes can disrupt our lives completely because they cannot always be anticipated. They may include such things as emergency surgery, losing a job, or an accident that leaves us or someone we love disabled. It could also mean something as devastating as a divorce or as exhilarating as receiving an inheritance. Unexpected change often disrupts our lives so completely that we are *never* the same again.

No Changes

This category involves events we believed would happen, but they didn't. Perhaps we always wanted to own a home but we've never been able to afford one. It could be that we thought we'd eventually marry, but we never met the right person. We might long for a baby but discover we are infertile. There was never a particular day when we knew these hopes wouldn't be fulfilled, but slowly the realization dawned. (These traumas are especially difficult to deal with. For a time there is an expectation, then a disappointment, which results in a deep longing for the change. When nothing happens, emotions take over, often resulting in discouragement, then hopelessness, and finally despair.)

CHANGES AFFECT OUR SENSE OF SECURITY

I've been a failure when it comes to adapting to change joyfully. Even positive changes bring stress to our lives. And changes we perceive as negative can rip our heart out, destroy our confidence, and leave us emotionally vulnerable.

In these two chapters, we're talking about the passion for security. So much of my sense of safety and stability comes from the feeling (real or imagined) of being protected, certain of my current conditions, and free from doubt or worries. When changes occur and my "safe" situation is altered, I come face-to-face with disappointments. Longings are born and emotions take over. I now have a choice. Will I decide on a ruling passion that will result in an honorable or holy action, or will I be influenced by faulty values and choose an inappropriate response?

In the last chapter we talked about the trials that come from our loss of security in the areas of *possessions* and unexpected *circumstances*. In this chapter, we're focusing on change and how it affects *relationships*.

Linda's Change—Unexpected and Unwanted

A closer look at Linda's responses when her ill mother moved in may help us to understand ourselves.

Linda's Expectation: She believed life would be easy, with relatively few stresses, as long as she was living close to the Lord.

Linda's Disappointment: Her mother's health crisis brought several unwanted changes:

- A live-in "house guest" who needed constant attention
- Tremendous stress in her marriage and in her family relationships
- A massive interruption in her personal plans for training and ministry opportunities

Linda's Longing: Her entire being longed for life as it used to be—normal!

Linda's Emotion: Linda's emotions were volatile. She loved her mother, feeling deep compassion for her one minute and yet almost hating her the next. She was irritated with her husband for "distancing" himself from the problem, then she'd become angry when he offered too much advice. Linda exploded with rage when her sister refused to take her mother, even for a weekend, saying her house was too small and she had other plans. Linda's emotions gave way to feelings of despair when she realized her life and her plans were suddenly—and indefinitely—"on hold."

Linda's Decision: Linda's values system had appeared

moderately healthy under stress-free conditions, but it contained a few holes that soon surfaced. The "myths" she dealt with negatively affected her ruling passion:

- It's my job to handle every crisis myself. (Can you tell she was the firstborn child?)
- I should give up all my personal plans to meet the needs of everyone else.
- I can't be happy if life is harder than I expected.

Linda's Drive/Passion: Since Linda's decision-making process was sifted through this damaged set of convictions instead of biblically sound values, her ruling passion was depression.

Linda's Actions: Her actions involved a series of choices that were misguided:

- Continuous conflict with her husband
- Begrudging care of her mother rather than loving service
- Withdrawal from all church and ministry involvement, accompanied by a defeatist attitude
- Viewing her sister's response over one weekend as a desire for total noninvolvement in her mother's care—as a result, she alienated herself from a sister she desperately needed.

Fortunately it's never too late to evaluate our longings and resulting emotions in the light of God's Word. Linda's deep love for the Lord, her husband, mother, and sister soon drove her to carefully study her initial responses. With the help of a Christian counselor, she was able to change her thinking and "rewrite" her convictions. Positive change didn't happen overnight, but she finally realized three important things:

- She does *not* have to handle every crisis herself. (She has a myriad of friends and family who are willing to help if she will give up her controlling attitude as "firstborn-solver-of-all-family-problems.")

•Being godly does *not* mean giving up all personal plans and resorting to the life of a hermit. Finances may be tight, but there are social agencies, non-profit organizations, and support groups in her city that can offer assistance. She might have to miss a seminar she longs to attend and alter the current extent of her outside ministry, but she does not have to drop out of life.

•She can be joy-filled, even if life is harder than she expected. This is tough, especially on her mother's "bad" days and on her own hormonal "down" periods. These times demand a sense of humor, flexibility, time alone with God, frequent mini-getaways with her husband, nurturing friendships, and an eternal viewpoint.

With these changes in place, her ruling passion has been acceptance, not resignation, and her resulting actions have reflected honorable choices that have brought glory to God and a positive challenge to observers.

EMOTIONAL TRIGGER POINTS

Often the first *recognizable* problem I have with change is an emotional reaction. Most of the time I haven't thought about the disappointment that created the longing that, in turn, prompted my reaction. That's dangerous—because then I automatically "read into" the situation and convince myself that *it's not my problem!* If someone else were a more perfect person or if these negative events hadn't transpired, then I would not be in an emotional upheaval. I then subtly blame other people for my resulting action without ever taking responsibility for my own ruling passion.

There are many emotional trigger points prompted by changes in our lives that can drastically affect our relationships. Some changes have great potential for "rocking our boat."

Change of Neighbors
My doorbell rang. Assuming the caller was one of the ten children per day who come to my house to see if J. P. is home,

I casually opened the door while picking the remains of an Oreo cookie out of my front teeth. There stood an attractive man with his hand outstretched, saying, "Hello, Mrs. Kent, I'm going to be your new neighbor. . . . I'm stopping by to tell you that we will be putting up a fence this weekend along the line that connects our backyard with yours. We raise German shepherds, and we'll be constructing a dog run. I certainly hope that won't be a problem to you."

I smiled and stuck out my hand. "Welcome to the neighborhood. . . ." My emotions were going crazy. While making polite conversation on the outside, I was screaming on the inside. My office window faces that property line! My bedroom faces that property line! My informal dining area and back deck both face that property line! A fence will destroy the beauty of the wooded area between our houses. And I cannot work on my manuscripts, have meaningful devotions, get a good night's sleep, and entertain company for a barbecue on my deck with a chorus of dogs barking! And what about my property value?

My comfortable little boat was being rocked. My expectation of peaceful life in the suburbs was being destroyed, and I longed for the continuation of life as it was—before the new neighbors! (Why weren't they moving to a farm in the country?) As this emotional stream of thoughts settled a bit, I realized I was jumping to conclusions and the action resulting from my ruling passion in this matter could determine the new neighbor's eventual response to my Christianity.

The "ripple" effect on relationships, initiated by something as "small" as this change in neighbors, could eventually involve:

- Stress between me and my husband, because he would probably not complain about the situation unless it became unbearable.
- A subtle "silent treatment" between me and the neighbors who "stole" my serene lifestyle.
- A wall between me and God because of my negative attitude. Couldn't He have kept it from happening?

Our initial emotional reactions are *not* sin. When we sift the emotions through our convictions, *we choose our own ruling passion* and the actions that follow. In the relationship struggles mentioned above, the potential negative actions will all be a result of my own ruling passion. That's where sin enters the picture.

Change of Plans

This type of change occurs almost daily and can be disappointing, but it usually doesn't cause a major upheaval in our lives. It might be a canceled appointment or a postponed visit with a friend or relative. Occasionally it's unexpected company. This type of change can be a relief or it can cause "a slow boil" if you like to live your life by a time schedule.

Change in Housing

A move, even a *desired* move, brings tremendous stress to most women. There is mental exhaustion regarding *where* to move, *what* to move into (house, condo, apartment), and *how* to take care of financing. Then comes the work of packing as well as determining what to keep, what to give away, and what to throw away. Once the move takes place, decorating may need to be done and furniture arranging must be taken care of—both involving more decision making and often conflicting opinions. At that point we need to make a good impression on the new neighbors, and it seems the stress has only begun. If you are single and have to take full responsibility for all decisions, moving can be even more emotionally taxing.

Change in Employment

Some experts are now predicting that by 1995, eighty percent of women between the ages of twenty-five and forty-four will be in the work force. Some of them will only be working in part-time positions, but these statistics tell us that a majority of women will be going through numerous changes in regard to job placement and in regard to relationships as the heavy stresses of divided domestic labor and child-care responsibilities are worked out.

Change in Marital Status

Going from single living to being married can be a shocking experience. Even if the changes that accompany marriage were desired, there are major conflicts when two people begin living under one roof! Soon "character flaws" and various tensions become evident.

All of us who've experienced marriage can identify with the story of young Susie. Her elementary school teacher observed her playing a game called "Wedding" during recess. Explaining the game to her teacher, she said, "I'm the bride, Sarah is the bridesmaid, and Jennifer is the flower girl."

The teacher looked puzzled and asked, "Well, then, who's the groom?"

"Oh, teacher, we don't need a groom. I only want a small wedding."

On some days the thought *has* occurred to me that marriage would be a whole lot easier without the groom! Our disappointments often create longings for a more perfect spouse.

A traumatic change usually occurs when a marriage ends—either through death or divorce. On the average, women live about seven years longer than men, which means many of us will face the major change of going from marriage to widowhood. The divorce rate in the United States remains close to the fifty percent mark, so half of all married women will become acquainted with the difficult changes that occur when a marriage ends.

Change in Family Role

There is almost nothing that changes a household more than the arrival of a baby! Suddenly this little twenty-inch-long human being, weighing less than ten pounds, takes over and expects you to jump every time he cries. Life will never be the same again! We run to them when they cry, and we wonder what they are doing when they are too quiet. Someone wisely said, "Children are like mosquitoes—the moment they stop making noises you know they're getting into something." Yes, motherhood *does* change life considerably!

Many women become "instant mothers" of extra children

when families are blended. This is becoming more common. For some of these moms, it's a tremendously difficult challenge to bring two families together, especially if the children from both families are to live under the same roof. The mother comes into the marriage with an expectation that her biological children will have a full-time father and that they'll be a complete and loving family—but often there are agonizing disappointments.

Change in Age

Each season of life brings new potential for living out our dreams and new opportunities for experiencing disappointments. With our youth comes a tremendous sense of optimism and hope. As the years go by, major decisions are made—to marry or to remain single, to take a job or to stay at home. When menopause comes and our biological time clock runs out, there is a special sense of the passing of time and the shortness of life.

For some mothers who have poured every bit of life's energy into raising their children, the empty nest can bring a haunting disappointment, sadness, and depression. Every corner of the house is filled with the memories of the laughter and fulfillment of the "growing years." A longing is born for the happiness of days gone by.

Retirement is another change point involving relationship struggles. A grandma told me she was so excited about retiring from her job so she would have free time to entertain her children and grandchildren on a regular basis. As it turned out, she experienced deep disappointment because the children came only once in a while on special holidays and then left after only a couple of hours of visiting. She described her lonely retirement as "one disappointment after another."

Change in Responsibilities

Sharon and I had lunch one day, and she said, "For the last two years I've been the chairwoman for a Christian women's organization, and I've complained daily about the hours of work I've been doing on a voluntary basis. Finally someone else accepted this position and removed the work load from my shoulders. Even though it was my choice to be replaced all along, I'm missing my former responsibilities. With this sudden change I'm experiencing a sense of loss."

This woman makes a statement for all of us. Even when we desire change, it's sometimes difficult to accept. We often suffer unexpected disappointments when people who once were dependent on us are suddenly shifting their loyalties to someone else. Richard Hooker says, "Change is not made without inconvenience, even from worse to better."[1]

Change in Health—A Personal Crisis

Most of us can cope with daily problems as long as we are physically healthy, but when we are coping with an illness or a disability, even small incidents seem like major mountains.

I have been grateful for excellent health and a high energy level for most of my life. It used to be difficult for me to empathize with people who endure chronic pain. Then it happened. A few years ago I grabbed a heavy suitcase out of the trunk when I was running to catch a plane. Searing pain tore through my back, letting me know that something major had gone wrong.

For months, on a daily basis, I woke up in excruciating pain. After a few hours of torturous movement each morning, the pain level was reduced enough to allow me to carry on with most of my activities. The problem was diagnosed as a herniated disc. There was medication that proved somewhat helpful, but for the most part severe pain lasted for a period of several months. The pain totally disappeared for a short while and then came back with a vengeance.

My Expectation: My subliminal expectation was for perfect health for my entire lifetime. I never consciously considered it an expectation, because I always took good health and a high energy level for granted.

My Disappointment: I had committed myself to an arduous schedule of retreat and conference engagements. Costly publicity materials were already printed and distributed for several seminars. I was determined to fulfill my obligations and assumed that God would take away the pain. But I was sadly disappointed.

My Longing: I simply longed to get up in the morning free of the "fire ball" in my lower back and function like a normal human being.

My Emotion: My initial reaction was the Carol Kent special: "Deny this pain and it will go away. If you work hard, it will take your mind off the pinched nerve and you will be able to carry on with life." But pain has its own mind, and day after day there were moments when hope was eroded by despair.

Emotions built up within me. Sitting in the office of an orthopedic surgeon, I begged, "Please give me a prescription that will kill this pain without making me drowsy. I do not have time for this ridiculous inconvenience! It's interrupting my family life and my professional life. I cannot stand being in bondage to this crippling physical handicap!" The doctor let me know my problem had no "instant" cures, nor could he promise the pain would go away. He suggested bed rest. I was furious!

Standing in the shower the next morning, I leaned forward to wash my foot, only to discover I was physically incapable of bending that far without crying out in physical anguish. I was hurting, and I was mad at God. Through my tears I screamed, "It isn't fair! I can't believe You are allowing me to suffer like this!" I felt humiliated and humbled when I had to have assistance with tasks as routine as getting dressed. Why was this happening?

My Decision: I knew from my upbringing that God's goal for each of us is to be conformed to the image of Christ (Romans 8:29), and I knew, intellectually, that pain was part of the process for the Lord Jesus and often is for us, too. Practical application of that truth was harder to make as I found myself in the grip of inflammation and pain that extended from my left hip to my ankle. Slowly, pain chipped away at my values and convictions, and I meditated on myths that were buried in my subconscious Christian mindset:

• I cannot be joyful if I'm not in control.
• If God really loved me, He would rid me of this pain.

- I must not tell anyone that I doubt the justice of God, because that would be a bad testimony.

My Drive/Passion: I chose a ruling passion based on the faulty values expressed in those myths. I decided to "tough it out for Jesus" for all of the wrong reasons. (In my heart I believed my denial of personal pain and spiritual instability was the "right" thing to do.)

My Action: This health change in my life caused a severe disappointment which fueled the longing for a body free of pain. When that didn't happen right away and I based my ruling passion on faulty convictions, my actions were misguided and displeasing to God.

My change in health drastically affected my relationships with other people. On the surface, to people close to me, it appeared that pain altered my mood, my tolerance of others, my ability to work, my sense of security, my feelings of self-worth, and at times, my relationship with God. But in each individual situation, I made choices based on my negative ruling passion. To people outside the inner circle, I appeared energetic, in control, joyful, and spiritual, with very few people guessing the physical agony I was experiencing. But my specific actions reflected my flawed values:

- I quit reading the Bible and found it impossible to pray.
- I went through the motions of ministry while simultaneously doubting God and feeling anger toward Him. This dichotomy in my spiritual life caused guilt and a subtle, growing depression.
- I became emotionally attached to a physician who understood my severe pain and had genuine compassion for my physical need. There was no immoral behavior or even inappropriate conduct between us, but my heart knew the potential was there because of my disappointment with God, fueled by intellectual chemistry and physical need for the regular doctor's appointments.

POSITIVE CHANGE IN OUR THINKING IS POSSIBLE

Fortunately, it's never too late to evaluate a flawed set of values and rewrite them with sound, biblical thinking. Evaluating my subconscious myths, I continued to discover huge "cracks" in my belief system that enabled me to change my ruling passion and direct my actions in an honorable fashion. My values were changed to reflect biblical truths.

•*I cannot always be in control of every situation in my life.* Because I still live in this imperfect world, my security will continue to be rocked by changes involving possessions, circumstances, and people. In spite of beatings, imprisonment, shipwreck, and persecution, Paul learned the secret that I still need to learn: "I have learned to be content whatever the circumstances" (Philippians 4:11). Changes are often unfair, untimely, and unwelcome, but that's life!

•*Just because God does not alleviate my current pain does not mean He does not love me.* The Apostle Paul's pain definitely was not alleviated, and yet he wrote,

> We are hard pressed on every side, but not crushed; perplexed, but not in despair; persecuted, but not abandoned; struck down, but not destroyed. . . . Therefore we do not lose heart. Though outwardly we are wasting away, yet inwardly we are being renewed day by day. For our light and momentary troubles are achieving for us an eternal glory that far outweighs them all. So we fix our eyes not on what is seen, but on what is unseen. For what is seen is temporary, but what is unseen is eternal. (2 Corinthians 4:8-9,16-18)

•*Admitting my doubts about God to someone else is not a sin.* Jackie Hudson writes,

> Christians who are struggling with doubt don't talk about it. They are ashamed of it. Or they have resigned themselves to living with it like they would an annoying headache. Tragically, many Christians today quickly

label doubt as "sin" or "unbelief." This adds guilt to the believer's already painful battle, and the condition worsens. For a sensitive "doubter" the struggle can be nearly intolerable.[2]

Hudson goes on to quote Os Guinness:

"What is the most damaging to Christianity is not that Christians doubt, but that there seems to be so little open discussion and understanding of doubt."[3]

Changes we view as negative often affect our relationship with God and our feelings toward Him. We are not heretics if we have doubts about Him, but *we do need to be able to talk to someone about those doubts.*

THE FIRM BASE FOR SECURITY AND JOY

We can count on three things that will last forever: God, His Word, and His people. Our financial security, our job situation, our marital status, or our health could change tomorrow—but some things *are* eternal. Malachi 3:6 says, "I the LORD do not change." Wow! That gives all of us a sense of security. Everything around me may change, but *our God is changeless!*

Besides God Himself, we have access to the emotional and spiritual support of Christian people around us. For those of us from the "I'll do it myself" mentality, it's a big step of growth to allow someone to help us—through physically assisting us or by giving us wise counsel.

There's an interesting story in Exodus about a battle between the Israelites and the Amalekites. When Moses held up his hands, the Israelites were winning, but whenever he lowered his hands, the other side started winning. We read in the Old Testament account: "When Moses' hands grew tired, they took a stone and put it under him and he sat on it. Aaron and Hur held his hands up—one on one side, one on the other—so that his hands remained steady till sunset" (Exodus 17:12). Aaron and Hur were support people who gave physical, emotional, and spiritual help to Moses in his hour of need. Who won the battle? The Israelites—it was a winning team!

When we face major changes as Christian women, there *are* people who can "come alongside." A caution is in order here, however. It's possible to be rejected by the person or people who seemed to be the best candidates to come to our assistance. Larry Crabb offers us some good advice:

> Disappointment can paralyze us so thoroughly that
> we won't move toward people for fear of getting hurt
> again. . . . But disappointment can drive us to hope. If
> we remain aware of all our heart longs for, even when
> we're badly hurt, then the prospect of one day being with
> Christ can become an alluring passion, a solid anchor
> that keeps us steady in the worst storms of rejection.
> A hope that keeps us going when we feel most alone will
> take over the central place in our affections.[4]

THE DOOR TO OPPORTUNITY

When our actions reflect ruling passions that are based on biblical convictions, rather than on distortions of the truth, our change points become opportunities for showcasing the power of God.

Washington Irving once said, "There is a certain relief in change, even though it be from bad to worse. I have found in traveling in a stagecoach, that it is often a comfort to shift one's position and be bruised in a new place." Irving was a bit humorous, but sometimes change does not make life easier. There's nothing in the Bible that says it will.

Is it possible to adapt to change joyfully? Tim Hansel thinks so. He says,

> Joy is a process, a journey—often muffled, sometimes
> detoured; a mystery in which we participate, not a prod-
> uct we can grasp. It grows and regenerates as we have
> the courage to let go and trust the process. Growth and

joy are inhibited when we say "if only," enhanced when
we realize that failures and difficulties are not only a
critical part of the process, but are our very opportunities to grow.[5]

Thanks, Tim! I need to remember that! Our lives are
constantly changing, and with those changes many new opportunities and problems are emerging. Whether the change is
one we have chosen or is one that we have no control over, it
can be the door to an exciting adventure through which God
can reshape the course of our lives.

PART FOUR

THE PASSION
FOR INTIMACY

SEVEN

PLEASE HEAR ME!
To Experience Human Connection

*We are born helpless. As soon as we are fully
conscious we discover loneliness. We need others
physically, emotionally, intellectually; we need them if
we are to know anything, even ourselves.*
C. S. LEWIS

Kate hesitated at the door of a local restaurant and then went in. The hostess led her to a window booth and placed a large menu in her hands. Sunbeams danced on the tabletop, begging to be recognized with a cheery response, but she wasn't in the mood.

Glancing around, she saw two women at the next table totally engrossed in a captivating discussion. Kate couldn't hear the actual conversation, but the body language said it all. The women were leaning toward each other, as if they were sharing important news. Their eye contact spoke of trust, interest, concern, love, and deep care. While one woman spoke, the other nodded, indicating intense listening. Occasional outbursts of laughter were a reminder that the lunch these women enjoyed was more than a serious meeting—it was a celebration of friendship! As they left the restaurant, they hugged briefly, and Kate overheard one say to the other, "I'll call you tomorrow!"

As Kate sat there, the loneliness she'd been experiencing too often swept over her like a rushing tide. These women had the kind of friendship Kate longed for but didn't have. Her sense of emptiness and isolation was like a gnawing ache that wouldn't leave. Bit by bit it was wearing away Kate's sense of connectedness and eroding her ability to think rationally. She felt tormented with the repeated internal message: "I'm alone. Other people can develop and maintain friendships, but I can't. The woman I most desire to have as my friend doesn't reciprocate. There must be a flaw in my personality that alienates me from people I want to be close to. There is no one I can call right now who cares about communicating with me at an intimate level."

I had met Kate at a Christian leadership conference. Her list of credentials was enviable; at the time of our meeting she was traveling internationally for her church denomination. She had classic good looks—from her perfectly styled haircut to her professionally manicured fingernails to her polished pumps. Her quick wit was balanced nicely with enough intelligence to give her "unstuffy" credibility. She deeply loved the Lord and had committed her life to Christian work. We "clicked" well during the conference and began writing to each other shortly thereafter. Occasionally she visited in my home, and during one of those visits she shared her intense struggle.

Kate's Expectation: She expected to share in a mutually satisfying "kindred spirit" friendship with Anne, a woman she selected as the person she would most like to be close to. She deeply desired a feeling of connectedness with Anne and felt that their personalities were ideal for providing all that was needed for intellectual stimulation, emotional support, and spiritual bonding. They lived in the same city and Kate felt the physical closeness was an added benefit for phoning each other frequently and spending time together.

Kate's Disappointment: Sometimes disappointment comes over a period of time, and this was Kate's situation. After choosing Anne to be her special friend, she spent months investing her time and resources into developing the relationship. She invited her to lunch, sent her "no-special-occasion" greeting cards with warm sentiments; she attended the piano recital of Anne's daughter, called her several times a week, and remembered important days with flowers and gifts. When they were alone, there were times when Kate openly and honestly shared her spiritual struggles with Anne. Later, when Anne was asked to direct the church Christmas program, Kate volunteered her time to put the program on her computer for easy corrections and access; then she assisted by caring for Anne's children during the program rehearsals.

As time went on, Kate realized that Anne was always grateful for her thoughtful gestures and was always warm and caring in her responses, but the relationship was one-sided. Kate shared her problems, challenges, and dreams, and Anne listened and seemed to care, but she never related any of her own innermost heartaches and longings. Kate sent cards and notes, but Anne didn't. Kate phoned and Anne was gracious, but usually Anne was not the initiator of the call. Anne made time for Kate when she "showed up," but Anne never pursued spending time with Kate. As one incident was stacked on another, Kate grew deeply disappointed.

Kate's Longing: Kate's heartfelt longing was for *human connection*, for the intimacy of a friendship that would be mutually satisfying. She deeply desired a friend who would be a supporter and encourager, but also someone who would be fun to be with during the lighter moments of life. Her heart sought a friend who would genuinely like her, find her intelligent, and desire sharing at a deep level. She felt a need for someone who would look forward to a phone call and a spontaneous breakfast out to welcome a new day. Kate's longing for the "togetherness" of a caring companion began consuming her thought life.

Kate's Emotion: Her initial emotion was anger. After pouring so much time and effort into a relationship, she felt she deserved more. The anger quickly swung to fear—fear that if Anne cut her off completely, she would have no one. Then Kate's emotions would bounce back to anger at this woman who was not opening up to her.

Kate's Decision: Kate should have realized that as a

Christian woman, her deepest longing for intimacy would never totally be met by another person, but her convictions and values had become warped over the years. She truly believed she was one of only a few people who longed for a close friendship and didn't have one. Her highest priority became easing her pain of rejection, and the actions that followed were a testimony to her faulty thinking.

Kate's Drive/Passion: If Kate's convictions had been rooted in her deep personal knowledge of the Bible, she would have chosen a ruling passion that would have allowed God Himself to fill the vacancy—perhaps through a different friend, or by a surprising change in Anne, or by a new intimacy with Him. She could have chosen to experience a greater fulfillment by offering her loneliness to Him instead of trying to take care of her own deep longing. But her instinctive drive was to lessen her own distress.

Kate's Action: Initially, Kate's choice was reflected by an action of total withdrawal from Anne, without an explanation. When Anne contacted her by phone to ask if she was all right, Kate's pent-up emotions exploded in a torrential outpouring of anger toward Anne. She pushed Anne further away than she'd ever been before.

If Kate's actions had ended there it would have been bad enough, but she immediately focused on another person to befriend in her desperate attempt to satisfy her need for intimacy. This time she was less patient and became demanding in the relationship. And again she pushed the newly targeted friend away by her attitudes and actions. By the time Kate talked to me, she had already destroyed four different relationships with women she had at one time wanted as her close friends.

INTIMACY DEFINED

Every human being has a desperate need for intimacy, but what exactly is intimacy? Webster tells us that "being intimate" has to do with familiarity. Intimacy is a close relationship that results from careful study of the other person.

To be close to another person in a friendship or marital relationship, we need to know him/her personally and experience "connectedness" with that individual in several areas.

• *Intellectual intimacy* makes us feel understood. Someone has the ability to reason with us on our own intellectual level and there are "sparks" of enlightenment and stimulation during our conversations.

• *Emotional intimacy* is the strong *feeling* we have for someone else. Usually the emotion is love and it gives us the connectedness of being tenderly cared for and totally accepted. Emotional intimacy doesn't always need words to be expressed. A hug, a squeeze of the arm, a touch of the hand, or a look can deeply express this type of intimacy. When we experience it, we feel cherished.

• *Social intimacy* allows us to feel like "part of the group." We join church groups, sports clubs, neighborhood gatherings, Bible study organizations, civic clubs, worthy causes, and business associations. Our mutual interest, work, or involvement bring us together with people of like passions, persuasions, and interests. Social intimacy does not make us feel as close to someone else as emotional or intellectual intimacy, but it does give us a sense of being "connected."

• *Cultural intimacy* makes us feel joined to people who share our roots, nationality, traditions, or values. Sometimes we meet people for the first time and sense peak-level communication because of our similar backgrounds.

• *Spiritual intimacy* can be ours on two levels: first, a personal relationship with the God who created us, loves us, and cares for us; and second, a spiritual bonding with individuals who share a similar passion for God, His Word, and accomplishing His work on the earth. There is an initial connectedness that stems from like faith in God, but true spiritual bonding evolves as a result of tracking each other's spiritual journeys, holding each other accountable for growth, and joining together to reach our world for Christ and lead people to spiritual maturity.

For me, an intimate friendship is a relationship with another person that involves many of the following elements:

1. A deep care and concern for me personally
2. A personality I enjoy (intelligence, spiritual depth, and a great sense of humor are a few traits I'd be seeking)
3. An active interest in and support of my projects and dreams
4. An instinct to automatically come alongside and help when I am in need
5. A spiritual bonding as friends (hard to define, but your heart tells you when you have it)
6. An "instant availability" when true emergencies demand momentary inconvenience
7. A commitment to each other, while allowing the other person to enjoy the freedom of time alone, other friendships, and individual personhood

Here's where Kate had a problem. She admitted it was very difficult for her to accept the fact that Anne had a deeper need for time alone than she did. Anne had difficulty functioning in her many busy activities without a daily block of time for solitude. Anne also had a personality that drew many close friends, and Kate was easily threatened when she overheard Anne speak with deep warmth and concern to someone else.

8. A compassionate heart that cheers when I succeed and feels my pain when I fail
9. A tangible support through communication (often enough so I feel valued, but infrequent enough so I don't feel strangled)

This is an area where Kate failed repeatedly in her pursuit of an intimate friendship. She called too often, sent gifts that were too large, and showed up on the doorstep so often that Anne began feeling pushed into the "friendship." Kate's lavish outpouring of time and attention was always a mixed blessing. She helped in many meaningful areas, but always left Anne feeling a little guilty for not bonding with her as an "only" best friend. There was something about Kate's desperate need for her that made Anne back off instead of coming closer. True "kindred spirit" friendship cannot exist when two people do not approach each other as people of equal worth and value.

10. An ability to lovingly confront me with hard questions that hold me accountable for spiritual growth and personal integrity

Kate shared her failings and spiritual frustrations with Anne, hoping that Anne would do the same and that their mutual sharing of secrets would bond them. In her desire for a close "accountability" relationship with Anne, she had difficulty waiting for the right timing. She found herself spilling out her heart in an emotional "child/parent" fashion, rather than allowing her and Anne to grow closer with each other as adults who had similar struggles and temptations.

11. A listening ear—someone *attentive* who will really *hear* me
12. A heart for God's Word and an eager interest in ministry-related activities
13. A powerful prayer partner
14. An affirming encourager
15. An individual who can expect all of the above from me without making me feel the "weight" of obligation if I don't measure up

Although both Kate and Anne were single, there was a difference. Anne was a widow with two children, and Kate had never been married. Kate's traveling ministry with her church denomination was very demanding when she was out-of-town, but her days were quite free when she got back from a trip. She felt a need for sharing with a close friend and for relaxation with someone else during those breaks. On the other hand, Anne's busy life of part-time work, car pooling for her children's activities, responsibilities with a neighborhood Bible study, and being chairwoman of a Christian Women's Club were time-consuming on a daily basis. When Anne was simply too busy with other commitments to be in touch, Kate misinterpreted Anne's lack of communication as lack of interest.

WE NEED EACH OTHER

Do *you* have someone in your life that meets the qualifications listed above? Okay, I admit it. I'm a perfectionist! My list may be somewhat unrealistic if used as a checklist for potential friends, but it's good for me to mentally review these characteristics. It helps me to evaluate if I've been taking more from others than I've been giving back.

All human beings have a different "comfort zone" when it comes to being close to other people. Some, like Kate, enjoy being surrounded with people most of the time; others, like Anne, feel suffocated if they don't have their own space at regular intervals. A few people need to be told fifteen times a day that they are loved, and as Tim Timmons says, "They married spouses who said, 'Honey, I told you I loved you when I married you, and it's in effect until I revoke it!'"

Many experts in communication are now saying that the average person needs at least twelve touches a day to feel loved, cared for, and significant. Regardless of our "comfort zone" differences, the fact remains—we really do *need* each other desperately! Even those who don't seem to have a big desire for *physical touch* need to be held with an *emotional touch*. The human race cries out—sometimes nonverbally, but still with poignant urgency—*"Please hold me!"* and *"Please hear me!"*

UNDERSTANDING LONELINESS

The need people have for human connection has been screaming at us in recent years with the rise in suicides. Jan Fawcett, in a publication titled *Before It's Too Late,* says,

> In studies of human traits that often lead to suicide, three words crop up again and again: loss, loneliness

and hopelessness. In many cases, an actual loss is involved—the loss of a parent through death, the breakup of a marriage, the loss of a job, the loss of health. . . . Hopelessness . . . is perhaps the deepest reflection of despair. When things are bad, people are encouraged by the belief that they will get better. . . . Loneliness and despair are frequently the result of loss and depression.[1]

Being lonely is the empty, aching experience of being alone, isolated, and "unfrequented." When we're lonesome, we have a desolate, unhappy feeling when no one else is with us. Sometimes we're just as lonely when someone else is around if there is no emotional, intellectual, or spiritual intimacy in the relationship. Proverbs 13:12 says, "Hope deferred makes the heart sick, but a longing fulfilled is a tree of life." When we hope for the intimacy of friendship and the longing is not met, we can actually feel ill.

Solitude, on the other hand, is aloneness that we *choose*. It's pre-selected time set apart for thinking, reading, spiritual renewal, or "regrouping." It can be the wonderful experience of "getting the wind back into our sails." Loneliness, on the other hand, is a type of suffering that comes from a lack of intimacy. Loneliness cuts like a sharp knife; when we see happy people interact with each other in intimate ways, the knife is twisted and the pain becomes deeper.

As human beings cease to feel valued by someone else, or when the communication system between two people breaks down, each person is then at risk—spiritually, emotionally, physically, and socially! "In one survey of 730 sex therapists and counselors, 85 percent said the number one complaint they hear is about the lack of communication in relationships."[2]

Some time ago someone placed this ad in a Kansas newspaper: "I will listen to you talk for thirty minutes without comment for five dollars." Did anybody call? You bet! Soon the individual was receiving ten to twenty calls a day. The pang of loneliness was so sharp that many people were willing to pay to talk to another human being for half an hour.

INTIMATE FRIENDSHIP—THE WAY IT USED TO BE!

Perhaps the most extraordinary example of human friendship in Scripture is the intimate relationship between David and Jonathan. At the beginning of 1 Samuel 18, Saul is king of Israel. David had recently killed Goliath, and he and Saul's son Jonathan had become friends. David was to become the king; he had been anointed by Samuel. But he wasn't to come into power until Saul died.

As chapter eighteen opens, Jonathan and David are entering a covenant relationship as friends. A covenant was the most solemn, binding agreement that could be made between two people—covenants date back to the days of Abraham, Isaac, and Jacob. The description of what took place and the language used in this passage make the close relationship between these two men very clear to us:

> Jonathan became one in spirit with David, and he loved him as himself. And Jonathan made a covenant with David because he loved him as himself. Jonathan took off the robe he was wearing and gave it to David, along with his tunic, and even his sword, his bow and his belt. (1 Samuel 18:1,3-4)

In Old Testament times there were no legal documents as we know them today, and there was a rather unusual custom of "cutting" a covenant that made an agreement binding. Individuals entering into a covenant relationship with each other would exchange their coats or robes as well as their girdles (belts). For most of us, a girdle is a device used to keep an unfortunate situation from spreading, but in the days of David and Jonathan, it was something worn around the hips as a symbol of security. Then they would exchange swords. It was like saying, "Everything I am and have I am giving to you because I love you. You take my enemies and I'll take yours. If anyone comes after you, they'll have to take me on, too. You are my friend."

After this they took an animal and literally hacked it down

the middle. Half of the animal was placed on one side of the men with the other half on the other side. After walking in a figure eight around the animal, they stood in the middle and pointed to Heaven and then to the animal and said, "God do so to me if we break this covenant."

This sounds gruesome to me as I read about it in twentieth-century America, but David and Jonathan were making an important point. It was like they were saying, "The intimate friendship relationship we have is more than a passing emotional commitment. It's binding, permanent, and absolutely undissolvable; I am committed to you."

The next step was to make a small cut in their wrists and mingle their blood. Then powder or dirt was placed on the wound to make sure a scar would develop. From that point on, every time they raised their hands to greet someone or to give a blessing, people would view the scar and know they had a covenant partner. The scar was also a reminder to love, defend, and protect their dearest friend.

The covenant partners then exchanged names and gave a statement of the covenant terms. They said, "All my assets are yours . . . and my debts are yours, too." They ate a memorial meal together and then planted a memorial to the covenant. Usually this was a tree that would stand as a constant reminder of the seriousness of their commitment to each other.

What Does This Mean to Me?

This old custom of "covenant" is a picture of the intimate friendship relationship that's ours because of Jesus Christ. One day I went through every step in the whole process of the covenant agreement and pictured the personalization of God's love for me . . . and I wept.

When Jesus came to earth, He exchanged His heavenly garment for human flesh. Jesus has become my Defender—if the Enemy attacks me, it's as if he's attacking my God: "The one who is in you is greater than the one who is in the world" (1 John 4:4). Jesus "cut" the covenant by giving His life on the cross of Calvary, and the scars in His hands are a permanent reminder of His sacrifice. In Isaiah 49:16, we read,

"I have engraved you on the palms of my hands."

He's given me a new name—Christian—and then He says, "All my assets are yours." They are listed for us in Galatians 5:22: "But the fruit of the Spirit is love, joy, peace, patience, kindness, goodness, faithfulness, gentleness and self-control."

Today, every time I take communion, it's a reminder of my intimate relationship with Christ. Communion is a memorial of His sacrifice on the cross for me. When I am alone—not in solitude of my own choosing—but in times of loneliness, I try to remember that I am in an intimate, everlasting, tenacious relationship with Him!

There are moments in our lives when loneliness knocks at our door and walks in—the uninvited guest who will not leave on demand. Then unexpected emotions come as our disappointments create longings for what we see in the lives of others. The trigger point for our loneliness can come in various situations. Loneliness can come when we watch a couple walk hand in hand when we're experiencing widowhood, when we hear our friend's description of a family reunion and know we don't have close family relationships, when we're alone for an evening and know there's no one we can call upon who will immediately come and fill our house or apartment with conversation and laughter. For Kate, loneliness came when she saw two friends in a restaurant enjoying the type of relationship she wanted. Sometimes loneliness comes when we hear a testimony of someone who is close to God, and we don't know Him or we feel far from Him.

Elisabeth Elliot has known widowhood twice. Her first husband, Jim, was killed by the Auca Indians on the mission field in Ecuador. Addison Leitch, Presbyterian professor at Gordon-Conwell Seminary, was her second husband. He died a slow, painful death by cancer and Elisabeth was alone—again! In her book titled *Loneliness,* she says,

> Loneliness comes over us sometimes as a sudden tide. It is one of the terms of our humanness, and, in a sense, therefore, incurable. Yet I have found peace in my loneliest times not only through acceptance of the situation,

but through making it an offering to God, who can transfigure it into something for the good of others.[3]

Our basic need for intimacy first must be met by experiencing a personal relationship with God Himself by accepting Jesus Christ as our personal Savior. From that point on, additional needs for "human connection" may come from friends, family, or a spouse. But in many moments when people disappoint us—and they will—we still have a Covenant Partner who says, "I will never leave you nor forsake you."

INTIMACY—THE STEALERS

In most cases we are the roadblock to our own connection with other people. Psychologists say there are several factors that keep us from being close to people.

Viewing Ourselves as Unlovable
When we feel unattractive or "dumb" compared to others, we have trouble believing that anyone would want to be close to us. We are quick to feel undesired or to misread someone's busyness as rejection. When we don't feel like a person of equal worth in a relationship, there is no possibility for true friendship.

Having Unrealistic Expectations of Someone Else
Our personal dream of a close relationship may cause us to demand much more of another person than he/she might be able to give. It causes us deep disappointment and is a constant frustration to the other person. (Kate had heavy unrealistic expectations of Anne, remember?)

Being too Busy
With over sixty percent of women in the work force today, our days are much busier than they've ever been before. Intimate relationships take time. Most of us want closeness without the investment of attention to the other person and the "togetherness" necessary for intimacy.

Struggling with Poor Communication Skills

Some of us *feel* deeply, but we have great difficulty *telling* someone else our heartfelt emotions. If we don't ever voice our needs, hurts, joys, and dreams to others, we limit the potential closeness. Family background has a lot to do with this. People who grew up in a family that talked, touched, and laughed together find communicating at an intimate level much easier than people who were raised by "non-touchers" who didn't voice their affection and opinions.

Comparing Our Situation with "the Ideal"

Women who do not have a strong family support system sometimes admit that it's easy to look with envy at families that *seem* to have so much going for them. On the surface it may *look* like someone we know has the ideal husband, the perfect children, supportive siblings, or committed friends. But what *looks* like the perfect situation from a distance often has just as much tension as a relationship that we are engaged in right now. In a roundabout way our disappointment leads to a longing for what we *think* others have, and it often leads to envy and depression.

THE COST AND THE RESPONSIBILITY OF INTIMACY

The intimacy I enjoy with my extended family and friends is sometimes deep, intense, passionate, and painful. At times the closeness opens me to hurt that I could have avoided if I hadn't opened my heart to those I love.

Within the last two weeks, I have heard from several close loved ones. One is going through traumatic marriage problems; another is deciding on a major change—leaving secure employment to go to Bible school. My best friend from high school is leaving the security of her teaching position to become a principal. A family member is in a business crisis. Another is celebrating a "just-found-out" pregnancy. Because of intimate relationships with these people, I feel pain, concern, sadness, responsibility, and elation.

Someone else voiced her hurt because I've been out of

touch by phone and letter. It cut deeply to hear this criticism, but intimate relationships are developmental. They need regular attention to be maintained. These tensions do not terminate close relationships; they're normal and necessary because we are imperfect people.

Intimacy in relationships opens me to emotional pain and fills me with joy beyond description. It's a paradox that defies explanation. My big responsibility is to quit trying to change other people to fit my definition of "friend." As I accept their differences, my life is more complete. Someone who thinks a little differently than I do adds a dimension to my life that I never would have experienced with my own narrow vision.

As I commit myself to the person and to the relationship, the fear of being rejected is reduced and eventually disappears. In conflicts I'm able to accept that we will never think exactly alike—and that's all right. As we spend time together, I let go of my demands for the "perfect friend of my imagined dreams." I learn to celebrate our differences while giving my friend "breathing room." Intimacy blossoms best when it isn't smothered.

A PERSONAL CHALLENGE

We need to realize that although we have deep needs for intimacy, we can also become "emotional filling stations" for other people. Taking the time to listen to people while giving them sincere, caring eye contact is a beginning. There should be a desire within us to provide personal concern and helpful resources to others, and even more importantly, lead them to the source of completeness—a covenant relationship with God Himself!

When we struggle with loneliness, we shouldn't be surprised. Life is filled with "alone" times. Through prayer, we can make our loneliness an offering to God. Instead of hibernating in our grief, we can get involved in the lives of other people. In the middle of our disappointments, we can choose a ruling passion that is honorable and holy.

Instead of expecting "instant intimacy," we can take Alan McGinnis' advice in *The Friendship Factor:*

> Deep friendship requires cultivation over the years—evenings before the fire, long walks together and lots of time for talk. It requires keeping the television off so that the two of you can log in with each other. . . . Getting close to a few people is more important than being popular enough to receive 400 Christmas cards every year.[4]

Intimacy costs top dollar and is never available in the bargain basement. It means time—to listen, to talk, to play, to pray, to ponder.

Reread the fifteen characteristics of a friend that were listed on pages 114 and 115. Prayerfully consider the people in your life now. Who is it God wants you to reach out to at this time? It will take personal sacrifice, time, and energy, but the rewards are great. Remember the truth of Proverbs 27:17: "As iron sharpens iron, so one man sharpens another." Are you actively involved in someone else's life, stimulating him or her to excellence?

C. S. Lewis described intimacy with others this way:

> To love at all is to be vulnerable. Love anything, and your heart will certainly be wrung and possibly be broken. If you want to make sure of keeping it intact, you must give your heart to no one. . . . Wrap it carefully with hobbies and little luxuries; avoid all entanglements; lock it up safe in a casket . . . of your own selfishness. . . . (There) it will not be broken: it will become unbreakable, impenetrable, irredeemable.[5]

My challenge to you is this: Take the time to develop intimacy with other people. The risk is well worth the pain! You can count on it.

EIGHT

PLEASE HOLD ME!
To Be Sexually Fulfilled

*It is difficult to define love. But we may say that in
the soul, it is a ruling passion; in the mind, it is a
close sympathy and affinity; in the body, a wholly
secret and delicate longing to possess what we love.*
DUC DE LA ROCHEFOUCAULD

T he woman stood to her feet, moved to the center aisle, and
walked to the front of the auditorium where I was standing.
Bursting into tears, she fell into my arms and blurted out,
"I'm an adulteress!"

I had just finished presenting the last message at a
women's retreat and had indicated that if any women in
the audience wanted to stay for a time of prayer, I would
be happy to remain and meet them in the front of the
room. The biblical challenge I chose to focus on had come
from Genesis 39. I shared the account of Joseph resisting
the heavy, repeated sexual temptation of Potiphar's wife in
Egypt.

Through the woman's sobs, she shared her story: "I'm
having an affair with the husband of my best friend. We go
to the same church, and I'm her roommate at this retreat. I
can't go on living like this!"

AN ISOLATED CASE?

Two weeks later I was sitting at my kitchen table finishing breakfast when the phone rang. I picked up the receiver, greeted the caller, and soon recognized a desperate tone in the woman's voice. "Carol, I don't know if you remember meeting me, but I need help. I thought you might be willing to talk to me. It's something very personal. Could I come to your home?"

The woman had come a long distance, but she arrived on my doorstep at the appointed hour. I liked her immediately. Her appearance and demeanor made a positive statement of intelligence, warmth, and spiritual sensitivity. We shared a bit of small talk. Nancy was married, the mother of three lovely children, and a very active church worker. I wondered what possible major problem a woman like this could have.

I paused momentarily, made lingering eye contact, and said, "Nancy, tell me, why are you here?" Her eyes brimmed with tears and soon her story came rushing out with the force and speed of a breaking dam.

Nancy married young and had children right away. She loved her husband and her life, but as the children grew, her husband became more and more involved with his work. She immersed herself in church activities and soon joined the choir. Frank, the choir director, was the husband of one of Nancy's good friends. Their children got along well together and the families often paired up at church activities.

Her emotions erupted like a volcano as she blurted out, "I honestly don't know how it happened. Maybe I was flirting a bit during choir rehearsals. Maybe I was lonely because my husband spends so much time at work. I've even wondered if I just wanted a little variety in my life . . . but it happened. Frank and I began meeting for a quick cup of coffee, as friends, following the rehearsals. It all seemed so innocent. Our families were best friends. . . ."

By the time Nancy got into her story, I realized this woman was on the verge of losing her husband—after eighteen years of marriage! Frank and Nancy's relationship began innocently enough, but soon their post-rehearsal choir dates turned into conversations in which they were verbally pointing out the flaws in their spouses.

For a while they only mentally reviewed the positive qualities in each other. But soon they began complimenting each other on personal character traits and attractiveness. On the days of choir rehearsals, Nancy found herself thinking about what she would wear that Frank would find attractive. She looked forward to his approving glance as she took her place among the sopranos.

Later when they had dessert and coffee, he bowed for a quick prayer of thanks for the food. He lightly touched her hand during the prayer and she flushed a bit, finally admitting to herself how much she enjoyed being physically close to him. It didn't take long for the "lingering coffee shop dates" to turn into a full-blown affair. I listened and then asked, "Nancy, how long has this been going on?"

Choking back the sobs, she muttered, "Off and on for *five years*." I tried not to look startled. She continued, "Many times in the last few years Frank and I have both confessed our sin to God, and we have stayed away from each other for months at a time. We've gone forward in church. Several times we thought our problem was behind us. Now we've been caught. My husband found out; he told Frank's wife, and now two marriages are about to be destroyed. Both Frank and I love our spouses, and we are sick about the pain we've inflicted on our families. Do you think there is any hope for us?"

Nancy suddenly looked up. With urgency in her voice she stated, "I still can't understand *how* this could have happened. I'm a Christian. What I've been doing is against everything I've ever been taught. I've been somewhat disappointed in my marriage—not *cherished* the way I'd like—but I've been *reasonably* happy."

I listened as Nancy described the progressive breakdown in her intimate communication with her husband, her growing attraction to someone else and its ultimate progression into a physical relationship. Over the next couple of hours, I intermittently asked more questions: "What led up to this immoral relationship? What were the danger signs? Why do you think it happened? Why did it continue after repeated confessions to God and numerous decisions to quit?"

She honestly didn't know. "Nancy," I said, "tell me about your thought life. What do you think about when your mind is not occupied with the urgencies of life? Have you ever had a problem with fantasizing about other men? What's the last thing on your mind when you go to bed at night and the first thing you think about when you wake up in the morning?"

With ease she responded. "Just normal fantasies. . . . I like to imagine what it's like to be in the arms of a gentle, tender, compassionate, intelligent, and attractive Christian man. Through my early married years I often thought about what it would be like to be physically close to my pastor or other Christian men I respected. I knew my thoughts couldn't hurt anyone else, and my dream world helped me to survive some of the more boring aspects of housekeeping duties."

Nancy soon admitted that the choir director she had become involved with had been the main object of her "imaginings" for many months before she stepped over the line into a physical relationship. The problem was not the product of one weak moment of temptation. It was the result of years of "practicing an immoral thought life." And she had never considered that it was sin.

As she sat in my home, safely removed from familiar faces, her "walls" came down and she openly revealed the disappointment in her own marriage and her longing for meaningful intellectual, emotional, spiritual, and physical intimacy from a caring spouse. It soon became obvious that Nancy's fantasies were not simply the result of being attracted to someone else, but there had been a severe lack of intimacy in her own marriage that eventually led to her current situation.

Nancy's Expectation: She believed that marriage to a Christian man would mean living in a happy and fulfilling emotional, sexual, spiritual, and intellectually stimulating relationship with her best friend. Nancy expected the intellectual intimacy of her courtship to continue after the wedding. She realized her husband did not grow up in a family that expressed physical affection very often, but in her optimism she was sure that would change after the wedding. She expected to marry a tender lover who would combine a caring touch, affirming words, a clean body, and a deep physical desire for her alone!

Nancy's Disappointment: Bill was an excellent breadwinner and always took care of the financial needs of the family, but early in the marriage there was a breakdown in the physical intimacy in their relationship. Every night after dinner they watched television, and Bill, exhausted from a demanding job, fell asleep on the couch soon after the news. Nancy felt rejected on many levels. Caring for small children all day left her starved for intellectual, emotional, and spiritual communication with her husband. When he hurriedly approached her for physical intimacy without first meeting her emotional needs, she was more than disappointed.

Nancy's Longing: Nancy's deep disappointment led to a longing for a close, loving relationship that would make her feel understood, emotionally needed, important, secure, physically attractive, and singly cherished. She longed for the sexual act of marriage to be the culmination of an intimate relationship on many other levels. Nancy believed that what she wanted was God's ideal for marriage.

Nancy's Emotion: When months passed and Bill's behavior didn't change, she felt "used" when he made love to her without first meeting her need for positive communication. His sexual advances stirred a progression of emotions: first, fear that her life would be miserable in many ways; second, anger that her husband seemed oblivious to her real needs. Finally, she was churning with desire for emotional, spiritual, and physical closeness with someone who would *hear* and *hold* her.

Nancy's Decision: She knew the Bible taught that marriage was a sacred trust between two people, and she knew she *did* love Bill. However, her convictions were clouded with distorted values as her thoughts lingered on her unhappiness, loneliness, and isolation. The damage to her spiritual judgment made her own fulfillment her highest priority—and she made choices that reflected her flawed thinking.

Nancy's Drive/Passion: Fueled by her daily habit of immoral thinking, which she considered "harmless fantasizing," her values system had become warped. If her values had been firmly based on God's Word, she would have been able to channel her need for romance and meaningful physical intimacy into a love willing to live with pain while she worked on a godly solution. Instead, she most valued being free of the anguish of not being cherished and decided on a negative ruling passion—*she would be emotionally and physically "happy" without the help of her husband!*

Nancy's Action: Her resulting behavior was the outcome of her ruling passion. She began mentally listing the negative characteristics of her husband while focusing on the opposite positive characteristics of Frank. Anticipating the choir rehearsals and the coffee shop chats afterward, Nancy began dressing to please Frank. She verbally complimented him on his clothing and accomplishments with the music program in the church. Reading "sexual innuendos" into friendly hugs and casual touches, Nancy spent her time fantasizing about romantic encounters with Frank. When they were alone, she told him of her intense loneliness at home and her deep attraction for him. A comforting hug led to a caress, which led to an embrace, which soon led to his bed.

"MOI? I'M A CHRISTIAN— IT COULDN'T HAPPEN TO ME!"

The highly publicized romance of Kermit the Frog and Miss Piggy brings to mind the very visual image of the gorgeous, voluptuous Miss Piggy batting her eyelashes at the camera in complete surprise while she purses her curvaceous lips and asks her most famous question, using her *only* French vocabulary word: "Moi?"

Sadly, I could fill this entire book with more true accounts of similar situations. In the last several years I have found myself counseling more and more Christian women in immoral, adulterous relationships with Christian men. Almost all of them thought it could never happen to them. Most of these women knew the spouses of the married men they slept with. Many of them love their own husbands.

The reaction of surprise that most women express when they experience adultery is much like the three-year-old's explanation for being in the kitchen, standing on a chair, eating cookies when his mother walks in: "I just climbed up to smell them and my tooth got caught."

By denying our deepest longings and pushing back our intense, passionate desire for intimacy, we wind up with actions that surprise us. Our emotions course through us, demanding romance, adventure, and "love"—and in our "innocence" (which is really denial), we're often surprised that we're capable of a negative ruling passion that results in the sinful act of adultery.

I have a little of "Miss Piggy" in me. Sometimes I'm all dressed up and I've curled my eyelashes and put on my pumps. I then flash my smile around to mask my deep insecurities and longing for intimacy, and I forget who I really am. In spite of all the Hollywood makeup, Miss Piggy still has a snout and she's still a pig! And no matter how much I'd like to believe that I'm a Christian woman of such maturity that I'd never stoop to immoral fantasies or to a sexual experience outside of my marriage, I need to remember—I still have a depraved, sinful nature at war with my new nature. When wrong thoughts linger, I so quickly gesture with a hand to my chest as I innocently query: "Moi?"

USA Today recently published the results of a survey of fifty thousand readers of *Woman's Day* magazine. The respondents confessed the following: "61 percent have been attracted to a married man; 35 percent, to a friend's mate; 19 percent, to their boss; 17 percent, to their doctor; 7 percent, to their clergyman."[1]

My first thought was, "But weren't many, if not most, of the respondents nonChristians?" Probably. But then I asked myself a couple of hard questions: "Have I ever been attracted to men in any of the categories listed? If so, have the men I was attracted to become an object of my fantasies?"

Several months ago the research department of Christianity Today, Inc., sent nearly one thousand surveys to pastors regarding sexual temptations. Thirty percent responded. They were asked, "Since you've been in local church ministry, have you ever done anything with someone (not your spouse) that you feel was sexually inappropriate?" The word *inappropriate* was left undefined and might have ranged from unguarded words to flirtation to adultery. *Twenty-three percent* of those who returned the survey responded affirmatively.

To some, that statistic alone is startling, but my surprise came later in this special report. Sixty-one percent of the ministers who responded to the survey said they *fantasized* about someone other than their spouse. Of this group, *thirty-nine percent thought their fantasies were harmless*. As the article progresses, psychologist Larry Crabb is quoted: "I don't think those who consider sexual fantasies harmless really understand the deeper, compulsive nature of sexual sin."[2] While an immoral thought life is not the only reason for sexual sin, the results of this survey are another dramatic reminder that we need to admit our gut-level longings for intimacy and learn the secret of handling our disappointments in the right way. Rationalizing that our thoughts are harmless allows us to be ruled by our emotions and deny that *we choose ruling passions that can be powerful forces for good or evil.*

A BIBLICAL PERSPECTIVE

A few years ago I had the privilege of working as Director of Women's Ministries at a church in Fort Wayne, Indiana. In any large church there are numerous couples with marriage problems, and it was a help to have Dr. Ken Nichols on our staff as the church psychologist. Ken often led marriage enrichment seminars, and his basic statement on physical intimacy was this: "Properly experienced within marriage and its commitment to fidelity, the sexual union brings a sense of well-being, complete identity, joy unbounded, perfect mutuality, freedom in responsibility, fulfillment of purpose, and an indescribable unity of being."

Most of us heartily agree with that statement. But even as I read it and do a mental checklist of my own physical experience of married love, I realize it's an *ideal* picture of sexual intimacy as God intended it to be—not the reality of my life! Often God's pattern is forgotten as we juggle home pressures, hormones, unexpected company, church responsibilities, and job stresses. But in spite of my imperfections and interruptions, *God does have an ideal.*

God Is the Author of Sex.

In Genesis 2:24-25 we read, "For this reason a man will leave his father and mother and be united to his wife, and they will become one flesh. The man and his wife were both naked, and they felt no shame." The primary meaning of "one flesh" refers to the sexual act.

God is the manufacturer of sex. It was created by God, sanctioned in the Garden of Eden, and meant to provide unity, intimacy, and pleasure. But because of the world's perversion of something so beautiful, many Christians have almost become embarrassed to discuss the subject of sexual intimacy.

God Created Sex to Be Pleasurable.

There are many subjects where the Bible speaks for itself very clearly, and physical intimacy is one of those subjects.

Old Jewish law stated, "If a man has recently married, he must not be sent to war or have any other duty laid on him. For one year he is to be free to stay at home and bring happiness to the wife he has married" (Deuteronomy 24:5). The inference in that verse does not indicate that he should be sitting around telling jokes for a year, but that he should be learning the intricacies of bringing physical pleasure to his wife.

The entire book of Song of Songs reveals the joy that should be experienced in the physical relationship of marriage. "His left arm is under my head, and his right arm embraces me" (Song of Songs 2:6). Solomon's description of his "beautiful darling" in chapter 4:1-7 is enough to make me blush. This man is in love! He continues in verses 9-11: "You have stolen my heart, my sister, my bride; you have stolen my heart with one glance of your eyes. . . . How much more pleasing is your love than wine, and the fragrance of your perfume than any spice! Your lips drop sweetness as the honeycomb."

Earlier in the text his lover says to him, "Your name is like perfume poured out" (Song of Songs 1:3). I might try dropping that line on my husband this week to check out his response! There's no doubt about it. God intended the act of physical, sexual love in marriage to be pleasurable.

God Expects Us to Meet Our Mate's Needs.

Another major biblical teaching involves the responsibility of meeting each other's sexual needs:

> The husband should fulfill his marital duty to his wife, and likewise the wife to her husband. The wife's body does not belong to her alone but also to her husband. In the same way, the husband's body does not belong to him alone but also to his wife. Do not deprive each other except by mutual consent and for a time, so that you may devote yourselves to prayer. Then come together again so that Satan will not tempt you because of your lack of self-control. (1 Corinthians 7:3-5)

Occasionally I meet a Christian woman who is devout in her practice of church attendance and Bible reading, but her husband isn't. Her way of responding to him is to read her Bible and pray ostentatiously in front of him and then deprive him of physical intimacy with her. She is nonverbally trying to indicate that he just doesn't measure up to her standard of spiritual excellence, and if he wants a loving physical relationship he'd better get his body to church the next time the doors are open.

In reality, she is using his desire for sex to manipulate him. Sometimes she does this with a series of excuses or even by the use of blatant rudeness. At other times she physically allows him to "use" her body, while acting totally uninterested and unfulfilled herself. It's as if she's saying, "God says I have to comply, so let's get it over with!" When we respond in this way, we defeat our own desire to reach our spouse for Christ. We also rob ourselves of the very intimacy our heart strongly desires.

God Created Sex to Be Experienced Within Marriage, Not Apart from It.

In the opening story, Nancy's decision to seek relief from her loneliness by having an affair with Frank brought intense grief to her life and threatened the stability of her family. The Bible gives clear guidelines and warnings regarding the physical expression of love with someone other than our own spouse. Hebrews 13:4 says, "Marriage should be honored by all, and the marriage bed kept pure, for God will judge the adulterer and all the sexually immoral."

In all my years of working with women, I have never heard anyone say, "The best thing that ever happened to me was the day I gave in to temptation and had an affair with a man I cared deeply about!" Even when a woman verbally expresses feelings of love toward the object of her physical passion, she usually admits that her immoral relationship has brought pain, confusion, guilt, spiritual failure, inner agony, and suffering to other people she loves.

UNFULFILLED EXPECTATIONS

All of us who choose to marry come to the altar with a hope chest full of expectations. We see our bridegroom at the end of the aisle in his perfectly pressed tuxedo, and our dreams are full of romance and passion. We anticipate excitement, unrestrained sensuousness, and chivalric deeds. But disappointments mount quickly when we realize that marriage to Prince Charming means cleaning up after his horse!

If we don't marry, we sometimes wonder if sexual intimacy is the epitome of all happiness and fulfillment on earth. If we do marry, we often wonder if this "intimacy in marriage" would be what it's supposed to be if we'd married somebody else. It doesn't take long for the Miss Piggy in all of us to see that Kermit is not a frog prince—he's a horny toad who is selfish and demanding, with little thought for meeting our real need for intimacy.

Somewhere between our expectations and reality we make our little list of disappointments:

- "He never really talks to me."
- "I don't feel cherished."
- "There's no romance in my life any more."
- "We never get away from all our pressures long enough to have fun together."
- "I don't remember the last time he just held me close and listened to my needs."
- "He doesn't seem to care if I enjoy our physical relationship or not. He's only interested in satisfying himself."
- "My husband has forgotten how to dream with me about the future."
- "I always thought I'd be married, but I'm not."

(Of course, all single women do not long for marriage. Most singles are living fulfilling, productive, contented lives. However, to the woman who has put life on hold "waiting for Mr. Right," there can be agonizing disappointments.)

When enough of our disappointments betray our expectations, we are open to temptation in the area of sexual immorality. Our disappointments create longings for oneness the way God intended it to be. When we don't experience that oneness, the Enemy often finds a foothold.

There are many reasons Christian women give for engaging in immoral behavior. Here are some I've heard.

Communication Difficulties

The Ladies Home Journal published a survey based on the responses of thirty thousand women. Most of them said they had chosen their mates based on sex appeal, but eighty percent said if they had to do it over again, they would choose a husband based on his ability to communicate.[3] A man who listens with compassion and carries on meaningful conversation is a great temptation to the woman who has no communication at home.

Loneliness

This problem is especially true of a single Christian woman who has longed for marriage. In spite of a fulfilling career and close friendships, if she has a strong desire for a spouse and God closes that door, there is a sense of loss. Loneliness is just as severe for the married woman who feels cut off from communication because her spouse is a workaholic or insensitive or lethargic. Temptation can become acute if an interesting and attractive man is available—even if he's married.

Intellectual and/or Spiritual Chemistry

This is the type of relationship that does not begin with any thought of immorality. It's usually with a business associate or someone you work closely with in a ministry situation. Since it begins as a friendship and you share common goals and a united vision for accomplishment, spending time together is a natural part of your work/ministry relationship.

The subtle nature of this "creeping immorality" is the most dangerous. It happens when two people begin working together on important projects that they feel passionate about. Psychiatrist M. Scott Peck has suggested that "spiritual and sexual desires are so closely intertwined that you cannot arouse one without arousing the other."[4]

In an editorial, Marshall Shelley, managing editor of *Leadership,* says,

> Researchers who have studied the neurochemical processes in the human brain have noted that the passion leading to spiritual fervor and the passion leading to sexual activity stem from the same kind of physiological chemistry. Though in distinct but parallel channels,

spirituality and sexuality are separated by a wall thin enough for a strange osmosis to occur; the energies get mixed up.[5]

Before you get disgusted and quit reading, stay with me! I do believe there is a godly way for men and women to work in close proximity, but the spiritual and emotional levels of people are very similar. When "creative sparks" are ignited in a work or ministry situation, there can be a subliminal cross-over to physical passion, often undetected at the cognitive level in the early stages.

Immoral Lust

This is an intense, erotic sexual urge directed at an individual, based primarily on what he looks like rather than on outstanding character or personality traits.

We normally think of men getting involved in sexual affairs for this reason; usually women need much more emotional attachment before physical intimacy occurs. However, for the woman who has been in several unsuccessful marriages and now views her fading youth and failures, there is an attitude of, "Let me live for today!"

Bruce Larson relates a story about an old priest who was asked by a young man, "Father, when will I cease to be bothered by the sins of the flesh?"

The priest replied, "I wouldn't trust myself, son, until I was dead three days!"[6]

Unspeakable Circumstances

I mentioned that this list could go on forever. My heart goes out to the woman who is married to a man deeply involved in a steady diet of pornography. A few of you have spouses who would just as soon get their sexual needs satisfied through masturbation rather than taking the time to meet your very real physical needs.

With tears, women who are married to homosexuals have shared their hearts with me. Some have no physical relationship with their husbands and long for physical intimacy;

those who *do* have a sexual relationship often fear they will contract AIDS.

On more than a few occasions I have wept with women who know that incest is going on in their home. For a time they deny it, but then decisions must be made which are often complicated by their intense love for their spouses and their children.

Others have approached me with the honest question, "My husband gets physically abusive when he drinks. At what point is it okay with God if I leave this man and marry someone who will be a good husband to me and a godly example for my children?"

Another difficult problem comes for the widowed or divorced woman who was married for years and enjoyed an active and ful-filling sexual relationship. The physical desires are still there, but she goes home to an empty bed.

God cares about our unfulfilled desires. If you are in one of these situations, God may use a variety of means to meet your needs in another way. Some possible sources for help are your pastor, a professional Christian counselor, a godly confidant, support groups, books on specialized topics, a mission of importance, or a revelation of God to you through His Word.

I know there's hope for handling our disappointments in the right way. Ruth Senter wrote an extraordinary article in a recent issue of *The Marriage Partnership*. She's a Christian leader, writer, speaker, wife, and mother, and she honestly shared her experience of being attracted to a man in a class she was taking. Nothing impure or immoral had taken place, but the relationship began exhibiting many danger signs.

Driving Ruth home from a class-related activity one night, Rick verbalized his deep feeling for her. After a painful internal struggle, she wrote a note to this man with whom she had experienced great intellectual chemistry. The note read, "Friendship is always going somewhere unless it's dead. . . . You and I both know where ours is going. When a relationship threatens the stability of commitments we've made to the people we value the most, it can no longer be."[7]

Ruth was able to make the choice that resulted in an

action that was pleasing to God, because her values were firmly rooted in biblical truth *before* she was situated in the magnetic field of intellectual and spiritual chemistry with Rick. The decision wasn't easy, but her convictions produced a ruling passion that honored God.

UNANSWERED QUESTIONS

Josh McDowell and Dick Day define intimacy as . . .

> sharing every part of our life with someone else. We all desire someone who will love and accept us for who we are, someone whom we can trust and open up to without fear of rejection. We desire love and intimacy, but we don't know how to find it.[8]

Why does it seem so difficult to develop relationships of trust? Why is a lengthy marriage the exception rather than the rule? Why do we fear rejection if we are open and vulnerable with someone else? Why are so many of our expectations of romance and physical love unfulfilled? How can we build a values system based on a godly view of intimacy the way God planned it to be?

BUILDING INTIMACY

The weekend had all of the markings of *romance.* A mystery trip. An unknown destination. Gift-wrapped packages. Anticipation built with every cleverly dropped "clue." It was the date of my twentieth wedding anniversary, and my husband had engineered a surprise. The well-kept secret turned out to be a weekend trip to Montreal, Quebec—a city we had visited on our honeymoon twenty years earlier!

After the flight, he picked up a rented Mercedes and whisked me away to our destination—an exquisite country inn along the banks of the Richelieu River. The atmosphere was perfect—an in-room jacuzzi, chocolate covered almonds, Perrier water and lime, topped off with a lobster dinner in the prize-winning French dining room. And the croissants! Ah, the croissants and the rich, aromatic coffee followed by a dessert of fresh raspberries and blueberries smothered in maple sugar and cream. The French-speaking maitre d' and hotel clerks added to the fairy-tale experience as they turned on the charm with "Bonjour, Madame . . . et vous, Monsieur. Bon appétit!"

On this "second honeymoon," Gene and I made passionate love and reminisced a lot. With a smile I realized the weekend had begun just as I was finishing this chapter on the intense desire we have to be "held" by someone else. I asked my husband what caused a deep abiding intimacy to grow between people. We laughed out loud as we remembered what clumsy lovers we were in the early days. Our awkward physical intimacy at that time definitely lacked skill and grace. We were quick to admit that learning how to handle our disappointments about each other in the first few years of marriage was much more important than an occasional glamorous weekend such as we were enjoying in Montreal.

We discussed the growth of relationships we have with friends and with each other. It didn't take long to establish a list of building blocks that have helped us "hold tight" to those we love.

Time
Whether it's getting to know a person or studying someone's likes and dislikes, or helping each other through a crisis—*time* brings a bonding of oneness to a relationship. Because of the demands in our lives, the sacrifice of time is a gift that tells someone else they are valuable! There is also a "comfortableness" that comes with knowing someone over a long period of time.

God
By sharing a mutual love for our Lord, His Word, and His work, we have a major "anchor point" that gives us a mutual goal, desire, and spiritual passion. If one of us (in a marriage or in a friendship) is out of close fellowship with God, our human relationship is affected. In a marriage, the sexual relationship is

always affected by the spiritual relationship. Praying together and sharing spiritual truths always builds intimacy.

Conflict and Resolution

Every close relationship has known the elements of conflict and resolution—or no closeness exists! We are not exactly alike, and our differing opinions will eventually become apparent. Where love exists, there will be a willingness to listen, to understand, to tolerate, to confront, to forgive, to compromise, to *resolve* the distinctive "differences" we have.

Tenderness

Making a careful study of another person allows us to learn the art of being gentle, compassionate, and caring in a "customized" way that will best meet that person's need. This tenderness is often hard to define. It occasionally surprises with gifts, special events, cards, or unexpected playfulness. Someone else senses my need for emotional or physical intimacy and meets that need in an appropriate and loving way that is perfectly suited to my one-of-a-kind personality.

"Holding Power"

Tencity might be the word to describe this part of intimacy, but it connotes that incredible oneness that is sometimes found in marriages and/or friendships where people support each other during physical trials, emotional distresses, spiritual upheavals, and personality explosions. This support and loyalty might not be deserved, but because there is love, there is a oneness. This tenacity is a holding power that survives PMS, infertility, marriage problems, loneliness, menopause, job stress, and old age. It's an intimacy that "hangs in there"!

Trust

My sexual fulfillment in marriage has a firm base in my absolute trust in Gene. He has made me feel that, apart from God, I am his all-consuming passion—his one and only partner, divinely appointed, to make his life complete. Sexual intimacy is a process of communicating love and affection by involving my whole person—mind, spirit, emotions, will, and body. When I present myself to Gene without embarrassment or pretense, there is a sacred kind of trust between us. I know I will not be laughed at or ridiculed. I will be held as a treasure and will know the feeling of being cherished.

The trust in a friendship, while not involving the physical intimacy of marriage, is still a bonding of mind, spirit, emotions, will, and the comfort of an appropriate godly touch, which is often expressed through a hug or a squeeze of the arm or hand. It's a way of saying, "I have confidence in your reliability and support, and I give you the same from me. I will 'be there' for you."

MIXED FEELINGS

In a chapter like this, I struggle with expressing in words what I feel. I believe the physical oneness of married love is an intimate communication of the whole being that is to be cherished, nurtured, and enjoyed. The building blocks for intimacy I've outlined above are the ideal—not a reality for very many women—including Christians! Most of my twenty years of married love have not been spent in a romantic French country inn. They've been filled with conflict and resolution, listening, sometimes giving in, sometimes "hanging tough," but always committed to a man I trust.

There are large numbers of married women who have never known physical, emotional, and spiritual intimacy with their spouse. Disappointments run deep. There are also many women who have learned the art of developing exquisite friendships that have met the need for human connection in a God-honoring way. But there are other single and married women who just want to be *heard* and *held*, and no one is meeting that need. God cares about our hunger for friendship, our sexual desires, and our spiritual needs. He created us as sexual, physical human beings, and He knows the passions and emotions that drive us.

It's never wrong to acknowledge our need. It isn't sinful to admit our powerful, driving emotional reactions. *Moi?*

Tempted by sexual sin? Jealous of someone else's intimate relationships? Fantasizing about my ideal life? Yes, *moi*! By admitting our disappointments, understanding the longings they produce, and acknowledging the fierce emotions we have, we can stop long enough to run our emotions through a Bible-based set of convictions instead of being irresponsibly "driven" by our longings and hormones! If we have established godly values, our ruling passion will result in a decision and action that is in line with biblical teaching and Christlike character.

Since this chapter has focused primarily on the longing for sexual fulfillment, it would be good to end with a picture of God's ideal plan for married men and women, beautifully explained in a letter written by Walter Trobish, missionary in West Africa, to a young African Christian:

> My Dear Francois. . . . Let me try to tell you what it really should mean if a fellow says to a girl, "I love you." It means: "You, you, you. You alone. You shall reign in my heart. You are the one whom I have longed for; without you I am incomplete. I will give everything for you and I will give up everything for you, myself as well as all that I possess. . . . I will wait for you—it doesn't matter how long. I will always be patient with you. I will never force you, not even by words. I want to guard you, protect you and keep you from all evil. I want to share with you my thoughts, my heart and my body—all that I possess. I want to listen to what you have to say. . . . I want to remain always at your side." If you use your sexual powers apart from this kind of love, you are preparing yourself for an unhappy marriage.[9]

PART FIVE

THE PASSION
FOR SUCCESS

NINE

I BLEW IT AGAIN!
To Transcend Failure

*Failure is one of the uglies of life. We deny it, run
away from it, or upon being overtaken, fall into
permanent paralyzing fear. Probably because of our
reluctance to face it, not much is written about the
anatomy of failure.*
HOWARD HENDRICKS

Exhaustion—physical, emotional, and spiritual—swept over
me like heavy fog in the early morning. After an intense time of
ministry at a women's retreat, I flew to Detroit Metro Airport,
waited for baggage, caught the van to the parking lot, and then
drove the ninety miles home.

As I opened the back door, my husband greeted me with a
quick hug and the news that old friends were coming through
town the next day. Earlier in the day they had phoned from a
vacation spot nearby and wanted to get together. The plans
were made. They would meet our family at church the next
morning and have Sunday dinner with us before continuing
on with their trip.

I groaned, then instinctively threw visual daggers in
Gene's direction and blurted out, "I love these people, but the
timing of this visit couldn't be worse! *Why did you invite them
for dinner when you knew I was getting home from a strenuous*

conference at this late hour? Couldn't you have been considerate enough to suggest that tomorrow isn't a good day? How could you do this to me? Don't you have any understanding of how tired I feel after speaking all weekend? You are a creep!"

One glance at the house assured me the place needed a "touch up" in order to properly impress the company, and I grudgingly scanned the freezer for a simple entree that could be garnished with enough flair to give me the *appearance* of a gourmet cook.

Landing in bed two hours later, I found that my mind and my body were on different frequencies. Hugging my side of the mattress so my husband would know I was intensely upset with him for putting me under this stress, I began practicing "the silent treatment," responding to his questions with grunts instead of words.

My body demanded rest, but my mind was swirling with a trio of thoughts: a review of the retreat, a plan for the next day's table arrangement for a Sunday dinner that would earn me a Betty Crocker award (and the approval and admiration of friends I *did* care about a lot), and a slow boil of ungodly thoughts toward the husband who set up the dinner I was too tired to cook! Sleep finally came, but in the morning the alarm sounded too early!

Running around like a maniac, I put the finishing touches on the house and meal. The clock was ticking and Gene was backing the car out of the garage. I called up the stairs to Jason, "Come quickly! We're already late for church!" When he emerged from his room, I couldn't believe my eyes!

With nerves already frayed by the events of the past twelve hours, I grabbed him by the shoulders, made intense, penetrating eye contact, and screamed, "How many times do I have to say it? You are not allowed to wear *white* socks with your Sunday suit and dress shoes!" My words reverberated through the hallway, suggesting an intimidating threat to anyone who might *dare* come within close proximity.

Jason's eyes filled with tears. Pulling away from me, he meekly responded, "But Mom, they were the only socks in my drawer."

Feelings of failure combined with conviction stabbed my heart. With the busyness of the past week, I had not realized the laundry wasn't done. On the surface, it appeared to be a simple misunderstanding, but his bodily posture and facial expression revealed a wounded spirit. The fierceness with which I had verbally attacked him was totally uncalled for and cruel.

Clutching him closely, I blurted out, "Son, can you ever forgive me? I've been yelling at you because I'm tired and frustrated—not because you deserve it. The socks are *my* problem, not yours! I'm so sorry."

I had blown it again! Fighting back tears of my own, I paused long enough to grovel in my misery. I had just flunked another Christian maturity exam!

You're a failure, Carol Kent! The words echoed in my brain. Jason knew it. Gene knew it. I knew it. God knew it.

DEVELOPMENT OF A MONSTER AND A PRETENDER

The above scenario changes, based on our circumstances. But married or single, we've all experienced the same situation. Combine fatigue, intense work or ministry, individuals we love, unexpected events or people, and suddenly we are magically transformed into someone we don't recognize—*a monster on the inside* (in our heart and inside the walls of our home) and *a pretender on the outside* (in front of people we want to impress)!

We often don't realize that our real problem is an insatiable passion for success. We long for people to look at us, adjust their glasses, step back, and say, "Now there's a pattern worth imitating! That woman knows her priorities, and no matter what the pressures of life throw at her, she has a positive attitude, and she looks forward, not backward!" When you add our Christianity to the whole package, we really believe our innate desire to transcend failure and to achieve success is based on a pure, spiritual motive. We want to demonstrate an excellent attitude and behavior that "moves on" with life—because that's what God wants us to do!

So if that's true, why am I so often a screaming monster and a skillful pretender! A quick look back at my response to unexpected company and my accompanying bad attitude gives me some painful answers:

My Expectation: After an exhausting weekend of ministry, my fondest desire was to "crash" at home. I expected to find a haven there, free from any demanding responsibilities. I planned to hug my family, brush my teeth, "hit the sack," and sleep, uninterrupted, until the next morning. I had envisioned attending the late service at my church, going out for dinner, and enjoying an afternoon of unpressured family time the next day.

My Disappointment: When I received news of the unexpected company, my expectations were destroyed. The needed rest was going to be replaced by cleaning, cooking, and "putting out the welcome mat" for guests I would love to entertain—*some other time!*

My Longing: At its roots, my longing was for an idyllic home situation, free of interruptions from the *real* world. My definition of this pastoral scene was comprised of rest, communication with my immediate family, a peaceful Sunday afternoon, and time to unwind after a stimulating, but emotionally draining, time of ministry.

My Emotion: After dreaming of my serene homecoming during the ninety-mile drive from the airport, my emotions were explosive when my expectations were shattered. Putting immediate blame on my husband for orchestrating this unwanted event, I lashed into him. With mounting vocal intensity, I shouted, "You have absolutely no concept of what it feels like to work this hard all weekend and then come home to find *more* work and unwanted guests waiting for you! You think just because my job involves jetting around in an airplane and serving Jesus that it's stress-free and I can come home with almost no sleep, slap on a smile, and act like the perfect hostess in order to impress *your* friends!" (They were *my* friends, too, but my verbal abuse wouldn't have been as effective if I'd acknowledged that.)

My Decision: At this point my emotions were quickly

sifted through my "values check-point." In spite of a spiritually successful weekend that included several positive responses to the gospel message, my values were distorted by severe fatigue and time pressure, complicated by a consuming desire to look "successful" in front of special friends we had not seen in over a year. The following are some of the myths I subliminally believed, which contributed to a breakdown in healthy, biblical values:

- I must be a perfect hostess and a gourmet cook in order to live up to the expectations of these friends.
- I must have my house (and child) in a state of flawless order and cleanliness in order to be perceived as the wife and mother these people have always thought me to be. This myth included a clause that read, "My son will wear dark socks with his dress suit" (to impress the company and make his mother look good, of course)!
- I cannot admit my physical exhaustion to the guests, because it might appear that my home and ministry responsibilities are not in proper balance.
- This stress is my husband's fault, and God will hold him accountable for being so insensitive to my need for rest!

My Drive/Passion: If my convictions had been rooted in a healthy, biblical foundation, I would have been able to see the whole situation with different eyes. Instead, *I selected anger as my ruling passion*—anger directed predominately at Gene for setting me up for this extra work, and resentment taken out on Jason.

My Action: My misguided, resulting actions were twofold.

First, I was a screaming monster and a silent martyr. With anger simmering like a pot on the stove, I used every opportunity to shout negative messages to the people I love the most—Gene and Jason. I chose to make Gene feel responsible for laying this burden on me. After I was "all yelled out," I assumed the "Christian" response to conflict: *the silent treatment!* My negative attitude was displayed with a disposition of rebellion, moodiness, ungodly speech, and finally withdrawal.

Second, I was a skillful pretender. After artfully engaging in silence all the way to church, I adjusted my "outer" attitude just in time to break into a warm, radiant smile as I stepped out of the car and greeted our dear friends: "Welcome to Port Huron! It's so good to see you! It's been too long! We're so glad you're here!" My act that morning could have won an Academy Award. I enthusiastically interacted with people and introduced our friends to folks in the church lobby. Faking high energy throughout the morning service and into the dinner hour that followed, I slipped into an outwardly warm relationship with Gene and Jason—and our company never guessed the rotten attitude that was behind this "snow job."

FAULTY CONVICTIONS—OUTWARD LIES AND INWARD RESENTMENT

Looking back, I wonder *why* I couldn't have lived out that scene differently. If I hadn't been such a quick reactor, jumping to conclusions after experiencing my disappointment, I could have avoided becoming an "emotional bulldozer" in my home! A values system firmly rooted in truth rather than success-driven myths would have enabled me to choose a different ruling passion. In retrospect, I discovered some humbling truths.

• The friends who called were not just "passing acquaintances"; they were such a vital part of our early marriage circle of friends that if *I* had been the one answering the phone when they called, I wouldn't have considered *not* inviting them over while they were in town.

• Had I looked more closely at the house, I would have noticed that Gene had vacuumed the place from stem to stern, anticipating my late arrival. There were a few areas that needed scouring to meet my perfectionist standards for company—but in reality, he had done a great job of preparing the house for our guests.

• On closer inspection of the refrigerator, I realized that he had also gone shopping, picking out a roast, frozen vegetables, salad ingredients, rolls, and a variety of items that would make meal preparation easier at the last minute.

Instead of "seeing the good" and "believing the best," I chose the ruling passion of anger after sifting my disappointment through my distorted convictions. My faulty values led to outward lies (pretending everything was great in front of the guests) and inner resentment (which was demonstrated in ungodly actions directed at Gene and Jason).

Most of us are gifted at pretending life is wonderful. Instead of being honest with people about the pressures we're feeling and the failures we're experiencing, we play "make believe," slapping on a mask instead of revealing our hearts.

Bob Benson, with hauntingly familiar words, wrote in *Come Share the Being* about how most of us "lie" when we're asked this familiar question:

> "How are you?"
> "GR-R-EAT! And how are you?"
> "FAN-TAS-TIC! How's the work going?"
> "GR-R-EAT! How about yours?"
> "FAN-TAS-TIC!"
> And everybody is so great and wonderful and super
> and colossal that you begin to wonder how anybody
> could possibly have taken time out for this (meeting).
> And that's just great if you're doing great and that's
> fantastic if you're really doing fantastic, but lots of
> times they are just words that shield and hide because
> it's not easy to say you're just doing lousy when every-
> body else is so great. . . . And I often wonder how our
> . . . church gatherings would turn out and how far-
> reaching their results would be if someone would just
> have the courage to say: "I'm not great—I'm not fan-
> tastic—I'm so discouraged, I'm about to die and I need
> your prayers and love." . . . And I wonder, too, how
> the world would be changed if we didn't think it was a
> mark of strength . . . to keep from showing our feelings.[1]

And I wonder what would have happened if I had admitted to our old friends that I was bone tired and a bit discouraged and too exhausted to cook. And how would they have responded if we ordered a pizza instead of having a gourmet Sunday dinner seasoned with resentment because of all the work it took to prepare? And would they have thought less of me if my house needed dusting and my son wore white socks with his Sunday suit because I hadn't done the laundry?

In all likelihood, we would have laughed and cried, admitting mutual failings in our personal and spiritual journeys, cementing an intimacy in our friendship that never could have happened in quite the same way with a "planned" visit. If my values had been healthy, I could have been honest. Instead of looking like Wonder Woman, transcending all failure, I would have been real and vulnerable and approachable. Instead, I was plastic, invincible, and "comfortably" warm while maintaining my distance.

THE HEART OF THE MATTER

I recently read the book of Matthew again and stumbled onto "The Seven Woes to the Pharisees." In the past I had always skimmed that part, wishing it was as moving as the advent of Christ or as inspirational as the Sermon on the Mount or as exciting as the recorded miracles of Jesus. But as I read this time, I saw myself as I really am. And the whole picture made me sick! The passage is convicting:

> Then Jesus said to the crowds and to his disciples: "The teachers of the law and the Pharisees sit in Moses' seat. . . . But do not do what they do, for they do not practice what they preach. Everything they do is done for men to see: They make their phylacteries [boxes containing scripture, which were worn on the forehead and arms] wide and the tassels on their garments long; they love the place of honor at banquets and the most important seats in the synagogues; they love to be greeted in the marketplaces and to have men call them 'Rabbi.'
>
> "Woe to you. . . . You have neglected the more important matters of the law—justice, mercy and

faithfulness. . . . You blind guides! You strain out a gnat but swallow a camel.

"Woe to you . . . you hypocrites! You are like white-washed tombs, which look beautiful on the outside but on the inside are full of dead men's bones and everything unclean. . . . On the outside you appear to people as righteous but on the inside you are full of hypocrisy and wickedness." (Matthew 23:1-3,5-6,23-24,27-28)

As God allowed me to see a small reflection of myself on the printed page, I noted too many similarities. In so many of my efforts to transcend failure and pursue God's excellence (with faulty values), I wind up nurturing negative attitudes, criticizing Christians who aren't like me, living by perfectionistic "lists," performing to impress others, full of hypocrisy on the inside while making "spiritual small talk" on the outside. The major difference between me and those Pharisees is that I already know God personally. I shouldn't have to play their game! But I do. And it makes me miserable.

I'm grateful that God does not have the same "performance expectations" as the Pharisees. So many times we disappoint Him, which must create a longing in His heart for the pure, unspoiled relationship He intended for us in the Garden of Eden. Instead of an emotional outburst of anger, His perfect, sinless condition leads to a ruling passion of love. And His action on our behalf?

The Spirit helps us in our weakness. We do not know what we ought to pray for, but the Spirit himself intercedes for us with groans that words cannot express. And he who searches our hearts knows the mind of the Spirit, because the Spirit intercedes for the saints in accordance with God's will. (Romans 8:26-27)

That truth encourages me! As we sort through our disappointments and experience our emotional reactions, our major hope is found in Him. If we start now by ridding our lives of the false values of perfectionism and invincibility, we can build on a solid foundation, grounded in truth, and choose a ruling passion that will result in positive actions of honesty.

DON'T LOOK NOW, BUT YOUR ATTITUDE IS SHOWING!

Whether we like it or not, even without words, people can often pick up on our inner attitudes. Most of us have never thought about how we decide on the attitude of someone else, but do we have an opinion? Oh, yes! Negative attitudes are often displayed by the person who has experienced a recent failure. The disappointment is fuel for the development of the attitude.

Lois Mowday describes what we see:

> An attitude is a disposition of the mind or emotions. Attitudes are expressed in a number of ways: the way you say something, the expression on your face, your silence, your body language, your behavior. Your entire presence conveys an "attitude." You don't have to come right out and say what you feel. You end up communicating your pleasure or displeasure, approval or disapproval, in a dozen different ways.[2]

When our disappointments lead to negative attitudes, we are approaching the other person or situation with a perspective that is unbiblical. Our focus is on "the person who did this to us" or "the circumstance that caused our problem." As we stew in our resentment, our vision becomes shortsighted. We begin emotionally reacting to the moment or to the individual causing our unhappiness, instead of focusing on a biblical viewpoint.

Because we're Christians, our negative attitude isn't always displayed verbally. If we've never taken responsibility for our own ruling passions, we feel justified and wallow around in our "pity party." Somehow we feel more "Christian" if we display our displeasure with a subtle facial expression, the silent treatment, or a pre-selected bodily posture. But we're fools to think we're only showing our temporary mood or mental state. We're revealing our spiritual condition!

The stark comparison is found in Philippians 2:5-8: "Your attitude should be the same as that of Christ Jesus." In the verses that follow, we're reminded that Jesus did not consider equality with God something "to be grasped." He was made in the likeness of man and became "flesh" for us, and finally He humbled Himself and became obedient to death on the cross, creating the only bridge we have back to God.

Failure was Adam's legacy to the human race. Our failure sent Christ to the cross. But, before that, our failure sent Christ to earth. I shivered as I read this description:

> How did Christmas Day feel to God? Imagine for a
> moment becoming a baby again: giving up language and
> muscle coordination, and the ability to eat solid food and
> control your bladder. God as a fetus! Or imagine yourself
> becoming a sea slug—that analogy is probably closer.
> On that day in Bethlehem, the Maker of All That Is took
> form as a helpless, dependent newborn.[3]

It's almost an unthinkable concept to envision God becoming man. One day I pondered the awful thought: What if Jesus had been so disappointed in God for making Him the sin-bearer of the world that He turned His back on our need with an "I don't care" attitude? What if? But He didn't. And because He didn't, we have the power to live by a godly set of biblical values—not in our own ability, but in His supernatural strength!

The same God who had the power to become a baby had the power to be resurrected from the dead. And that same God lives in me today! Because of Jesus' ruling passion of love, Adam's legacy of failure has been overruled.

THE PASSION TO TRANSCEND FAILURE

I hate to fail! I am currently rewriting the entire manuscript for this book. It's a project that I've been tempted to give up on more than once. It's forced me to reveal personal secrets and painful memories. I've struggled with attitude problems. When completed, it will open me to fresh wounds at the hand of the critic's pen. This project has taken a year and a half of most of my leisure time—and even when I'm engaged in other activities, my mind is weighed down with the lack of closure on a job that isn't finished. At times it feels like there is no end. Is any project worth this much sacrifice?

So *why* am I still writing? If you've ever been in Christian publishing, you know it isn't for the royalties! I'd like to think I'm driven to write because I believe the content of this book will glorify God and give us, as Christian women, a desire to evaluate our disappointments in the light of biblical values, thus resulting in honorable and holy actions.

That's a portion of my motive, but there's another part of me that cannot bear the thought of failure. I signed my name to a contract, and I feel the mixed blessing of obligation and opportunity connected with that. Quitting now would mean admitting failure—to myself, to those in my circle of friends, to the publisher, and to God.

With the messages in today's culture shouting success clichés at us, it's sometimes hard to admit our failures and human frailties to one another. I want the people around me to think I'm successful. I wish I were more spiritual than that, but we all tend to get caught up in trying to obtain favorable results that announce to the world that we've accomplished something we planned or attempted.

When we fail, there's a sense of losing power or strength. We feel somehow "insufficient," not good enough, and unsuccessful. (It's a horrible feeling to know you're trying your hardest and still doing "C+" work in a world of "A+" competitors!) When depressing thoughts of potential failure swoop down on us, we always make a choice.

Our expectations are unfulfilled, disappointment sets in, and longings are born. Emotions swing back and forth. If our Christian values are strong and vital, our ruling passion will be an attitude that is honoring to God and an ongoing action that brings Him glory. But if those values have been weakened by exhaustion, injustice, pretending, and alienation from God Himself, a negative attitude will prevail, resulting in actions that grieve the God who made us.

Someone once said, "Attitudes are the quiet judgments that shape our lives; they mold the form that living takes."

Will we experience feelings of failure again? No doubt! Will we battle with negative attitudes in the future? Chances are pretty good that next Sunday morning we'll have another opportunity to do battle with the Enemy and determine a resulting action. But in the middle of our struggle, we must remember Christmas Day!

TEN

SELF-ACTUALIZATION?
To Be All I Can Be

*If I'm not free to fail, I'm not free to take risks,
and everything in life that's worth doing involves a
willingness to take a risk and involves the risk
of failure. . . . I have to try, but I do not have to
succeed. Following Christ has nothing to do with
success as the world sees success.*
MADELEINE L'ENGLE

Women were stuffed everywhere in the small hotel room. My stomach hurt from laughing so hard. But beneath the laughter there were hard questions. And later, some of the women wept.

It was the midpoint of a weekend conference, and a few participants had asked if we could get together and talk about the changing roles of Christian women in today's society. I was tired, but the eager faces of these intelligent young women whetted my appetite for a challenging discussion. The topic sounded slightly controversial, and I knew it would be a lively dialogue with strong opinions being expressed.

Word spread quickly that my room would be "the gathering place" for this informal meeting, and the women kept coming in, sitting on the beds or cross-legged on the floor. Others dangled their legs from the dresser. I loved their informality and unpretentious manner. Most of them were youthful college graduates. Single. Married. A few were young moms. *Neat group,* I thought.

The initiators of the meeting assumed leadership. They began with a brief summary of "the changing times" for women in America, humorously dramatizing society's message to women reaching maturity in each of the following decades.

The '40s and '50s: "Be a perfect housewife and mother. Have milk and cookies ready for your children after school. Cook wonderful dinners. Support your husband's career, and have no ambitions outside your home besides the PTA and the local church."

The '60s and '70s: "Escape domestic drudgery and get a job! But more than a job, pursue a *career*. Consider postponing marriage and children for a few years. If you *do* marry, let your family be more independent."

The '80s and '90s: "You can have it all! Honey, you can bring home the bacon *and* fry it up in a pan. After your power lunch and business meetings, you can exercise at the health club and still be home in time to be a loving wife and mother. If you're a Christian, God and church need to be in this picture too—somewhere near the top—but *you're a 'woman of the '90s' and you are the image of success!*"

Suddenly the mood in the room changed drastically and the women got very serious. The unplanned, spontaneous way this group had come together, combined with the relaxation of laughter, sparked peak-level communication and bottom-line honesty. One by one these young women began voicing their various frustrations and questions. Hard questions. Deep frustrations.

• "I'm thirty-two years old and I'm still trying to figure out what I want to *be* when I grow up! Being single doesn't allow me the buffer of another person helping with household expenses while I investigate other job opportunities. I long to be in a work or ministry situation that will allow me to fully develop my potential. My deepest desire is to be all that I can be. It's like there's something inside of me that's dying to come out. I know I have potential that hasn't been tapped yet. Sometimes I feel like screaming! I'm locked in a dead-end job because I'm afraid to risk failure—and bankruptcy! What should I do?"

• "I'm afraid of the word *average*. I look at my mother and my older sisters and they live from one day to the next without any visible thought or planning. My worst fear is that I'll get to be old without having reached my greatest potential. I don't have to be *famous* to feel fulfilled, but *I do want to reach beyond the ordinary and excel at something*. Is that unspiritual?"

• "I just passed the bar exam this year. My parents sacrificed to put me through undergraduate school and then law school. My husband has a good job—nothing close to my earning potential in law—but his employment *does* meet our basic living expenses and a little more. Now that I'm the mother of two small children, becoming a practicing attorney has lost its appeal. I believe there's nothing more important I could do right now than being with my kids, but I'm feeling tremendous pressure because of my parents' expectations. We're all Christians, and they want me to be a good mother, too, but they can't understand why I would consider *wasting* all of that time and money on my education if I'm not going to *use* it. Are my desires wrong? I'm starting to feel resentment toward my parents."

• "My engagement was announced last week, and in three months I'll be married to a seminary student. My degree is in business administration, and I'm planning a career in marketing and sales. I think I can be a pastor's wife *and* a businesswoman, but I keep running into people who are shocked with that thought. I know several pastor's wives who are teachers or nurses, but the thought of a pastor's wife in business seems to scare people. Why shouldn't I be allowed to pursue what I'm best at without struggling under the expectations of individuals who define the role of the pastor's wife differently than I do? This makes me so angry!"

• "I feel trapped. I married at eighteen, had four children by the time I was twenty-five, and have never had an opportunity to go to college. Whenever I'm with a group of women like you, I feel inadequate. One of my earliest memories dates back to third grade when I gave an incorrect answer to the teacher's question, and in front of the whole class she said, 'Why can't you be as good a student as your sister was?' It seems like I've always felt inferior. It usually terrifies me to be with educated people, but I want to change. What can I do?"

• "Prestige and power are not all that important to me, but I *do* have a longing to know if I'm living up to the potential that God placed in me. I've been a secretary in a downtown office for the last four years, but I've been experiencing 'creative restlessness.' Is there something else I should be doing with my life? I'm interested in so many other things. How do I know if God wants me to be content where I am or if He wants me to step out in a new direction, even if it feels risky? I feel disappointment in myself for not finding my work as fulfilling as I thought it would be."

UNFULFILLED EXPECTATIONS

These women were voicing serious questions. And I didn't have answers. But I sure did identify with them! Disappointments had given birth to longings, and emotions were being felt and expressed. Most of the women were just beginning to run those disappointments through their values and convictions. They had not yet decided on a ruling passion and a resulting action, but they were longing for a sense of direction.

I mentally ran through their list of disappointments:

• Desiring to try different employment, but being held back by economic limitations and fear of failure
• Hoping to do something extraordinary with time and talents, but feeling "average"
• Longing for parents to accept a personal choice to be "self-actualized" at home, but being disappointed by their negative response
• Wanting Christians to understand the compatibility of a business career and the role as a pastor's wife, but feeling rejected and judged

- Wishing for educational opportunities and the resulting self-esteem, but being held back by the constraints of time, responsibilities, and fear
- Expecting to be in a fulfilling job, but feeling unchallenged and a bit unspiritual for being restless

SELF-ACTUALIZATION?

How in the world are we supposed to combine our Christianity and our deep desire for self-actualization? Truthfully, I don't even like the word *self-actualization.* It sounds like a workshop topic at a motivational conference. Yet, if I'm honest, I know I have a longing to discover who the real "me" is. Most of us wonder if we're working at what we're best at or if we should be exploring other possibilities.

We long to have answers to key questions:

- What are my greatest assets?
- What are my personal limitations?
- How can I be most effective as a woman in my sphere of influence?
- If I'm comfortable with my choices, should I worry about the disapproval of other people?

Even as we review these questions, we wonder: Is this kind of thinking too self-centered? Maybe God wants us to deny those thoughts and feelings and have more "spiritual" aspirations.

A VIVID MEMORY

Monday through Friday my life was always the same. Blackboard. Overhead projector. Students. Teachers' lounge. Lesson plans. *I was sick of it!* And I felt guilty for being sick of it.

Four years earlier I was so full of expectations and anticipation. I had just received my Bachelor of Science degree in Speech Education. I was going to be the best English and speech teacher that ever hit Fremont Junior High School! Students were going to enjoy my classes, and I knew they would fall in love with nouns, verbs, gerunds, and participles. All they needed was an enthusiastic, well-prepared teacher and the right motivation.

I had it all figured out. The public school classroom was going to be my arena for being "salt" in the real world. The teaching would be educationally excellent—but students would be drawn to the Lord as a result of being in my classes. It was my opportunity to be a Christian woman of influence in my chosen profession.

Now, just four years later, I was a restless, unsatisfied clock-watcher who secretly wished I'd majored in something other than education. I was deeply disappointed in myself for feeling this way! The other teachers in my building had presented me with a plaque I proudly hung on my wall: "OUTSTANDING BEGINNING SECONDARY TEACHER." My students honored me at the last assembly of the year by voting me "Teacher of the Year"! On the surface I looked successful. *Why was I so discontent?*

ANALYZING OUR PASSION FOR SUCCESS

We all have a desire to transform from an "average" woman into an "extraordinary" woman. We're curious to know what our potential really is. Inside we have a longing to know *who we are* and *to be our most true self.* Success, for most of us, is more than accomplishing something we planned or attempted. It's finding our unique niche in this world and then fulfilling our goals with all our might. We long to feel great about the results and to have the affirmation of significant people. Without that approval—from ourselves and others—we often don't *feel* successful.

In a sense, the women who gathered in my hotel room the night of the weekend conference were expressing the same disappointment I was feeling after four years of teaching. In spite of our different stages of life, we had much in common.

Our Expectation: If we were Christians at the time we

approached adulthood, most of us believed that, with God's help, we would make a decision on a career or vocation that would make us happy and fulfilled for a lifetime. We knew we should pray hard, keep our eyes open for divine guidance, and then act. We expected the result to be personal fulfillment in a life situation that allowed us to live up to our greatest potential. This would also be accompanied by the approval and affirmation of people close to us, adding to our feeling of success. When I signed my first teaching contract, I *knew* my expectation would be met.

Our Disappointment: For many of us, disappointment comes over a period of time. I was surprised that my fourth year of teaching wasn't as fulfilling as the first few years. With all the time and money spent on my education, combined with my desire to make a spiritual difference in the lives of my students, I was disappointed in myself for being discontented. I was also disappointed in the teaching profession for not being challenging enough to keep me interested.

Our Longing: At the root level, our deepest longing is for "the absence of restlessness," to be satisfied with God's purpose for our lives. On the surface, our longing is for self-actualization—not putting ourselves forward, but finding out that which we do best. We long to discover the all-satisfying, custom-made spot to showcase our God-given talents in a way that will bring personal and spiritual fulfillment.

Our Emotions: At this point our emotions go wild! I walked into my empty classroom one day, closed the door, surveyed the room, and shouted: *"If I am still in this schoolroom doing the same thing twenty-five years from now, I will go crazy!"* On my knees a few days later, I prayed, "Lord, I love my students. I know You've used me in a unique way to reach several kids in this school for Christ. I do not understand my current frustration. I feel like You've designed me to do something else. I hate myself for not being satisfied with the job I already have! *Please help me!"*

Our Decision: Fortunately, we have a "convictions clearinghouse" that will always help us to make a decision on our ruling passion. In our hearts we know that God has gifted us and that we're created in His image with incredible potential to do something extraordinary with our lives. If those convictions are built on biblical truth, the end result will honor God. But sometimes those convictions are damaged by life's negative events and disillusionment with God. More often, the problem is our own faulty thinking. Some of the myths we accept as truth are these:

- I am only as good as my job description.
- Because I'm a Christian, God will always make me happy in my work.
- If other people don't approve of my choices, I must be wrong.
- God will love me more if I'm "above average."
- If I got poor grades as a kid, I'm unintelligent.
- If I try something new and fail, I'm out of God's will.
- Feeling creative restlessness in my work means I'm discontented with God.

Our Drive/Passion: Our ruling passion will always determine our action. After searching my heart and feeling a tremendous struggle within, my ruling passion was determined. I would practice contentment in my job situation, not based on my feelings (which were negative), but based on my trust in God (the same God I had trusted in the past when I *agreed* with His leading).

Sometimes we have more than one battle with the determination of a ruling passion. On "bad days" in the classroom when my energy level was low and my heart was longing to be doing something else, I struggled *again and again.* Going back through my convictions, I had to daily choose my ruling passion. Would it be contentment or dissatisfaction? The condition of my spiritual health was always the determining factor in my ruling passion.

Our Action: It was true for most of the women gathered in the hotel room that their action had not yet been determined. For me, my action was almost humorous, because it outwardly didn't seem to be an action. But it was. My action was to *wait* (with my eyes open), while practicing contentment.

WAITING—WITH IMPATIENCE

Waiting rooms. I don't like them. They always make me feel controlled by a higher authority. Someone else has power over my carefully planned schedule for the day. And do they care? Of course not! If they did, they wouldn't overschedule like they do. Right?

And sometimes when I'm sitting around waiting for God's direction, longing to use my potential in a productive way for His glory, and no opportunity manifests itself, I'm disappointed. On the surface it seems like He doesn't care. Everything seems "status quo." Boring. Nothing exciting on the horizon.

If my values are full of holes because of my disappointment with God, my imagination takes over. Flashing before me, I see the titles of books that will promise me quicker, more successful results than God seems interested in providing:

- *The Success System that Never Fails*
- *Pulling Your Own Strings*
- *The Magic of Thinking Big*
- *How I Raised Myself from Failure to Success*
- *You Can if You Think You Can*
- *Think and Grow Rich*

Last week I punched the television remote control button and flipped on a cable program. The advertisement on the screen was promoting a new videotape I could order for $19.95. The title made me laugh out loud—"Play the Piano Overnight!" The commercial featured the testimonial of a celebrity and demonstrations of people who claimed to have used this "secret formula" to master the keyboard in one day. I was tempted to call my mother to tell her she had wasted hundreds of dollars on piano lessons, to say nothing of my own wasted hours of agonizing practice through the years. *Why didn't somebody tell me there was a way to avoid waiting?*

(The advertisement wasn't on this week. Maybe the Better Business Bureau caught up with them! Could it be that there's no *real* way to avoid waiting for some things?)

WAITING—WITH EXPECTANT HOPE

As a child I had memorized Isaiah 40:31 (KJV):

> But they that wait upon the LORD shall renew their strength; they shall mount up with wings as eagles; they shall run, and not be weary; and they shall walk, and not faint.

One day while reading the same verse in the NIV translation, I made a wonderful discovery. It began, "But those who hope in the LORD will renew their strength. They will soar on wings like eagles." That was the answer for which I had been looking. For the Christian, "waiting" is not the opposite of progress or the barrier to success. *Waiting* is *expectant hope*.

God created us with an overwhelming desire to *soar*. Our desire to develop and use every ounce of potential He's placed in us is not egotistical. He designed us to be tremendously productive and "to mount up with wings like eagles," realistically dreaming of what He can do with our potential.

The next day Jason was going to the library, and I asked him to bring home a book on eagles. I chuckled when he came through the door with an elementary reader, written on the fourth-grade level, titled *Raccoons and Eagles*. But my amusement soon turned to fascination as I studied the process involved in soaring:

> The eagle's bones are hollow and its entire skeleton weighs only half as much as its approximately 7,000 feathers. The 15 pound weight of the bird along with its huge wingspan of six or seven feet makes it hard to get up in the air in its own strength.
>
> But the weight that makes an eagle clumsy on

the ground will, in the air, give it the stability and lift needed for prolonged soaring and gliding. An eagle's bulk makes flapping flight hard work, so she finds a strong updraft (a wind deflected upward by a hillside), spreads her broad, flat wings, and rides, carried by the power of something other than herself. The eagle is able to soar effortlessly for hours on these rising "thermals," without ever flapping its wings.[1]

So many times in our lives we hold back from trying something new because of fear of failure. In our hearts, we long to soar, but then we think about the practical side of things. What about the constraints of time, money, responsibilities, and other people's negative opinions about what we're attempting? Yet, in a corner of our most true self, there's an eagle waiting for a rising thermal, looking for the courage to spread those wings, and scared to death of failing. So instead of soaring, held up by the power of the Almighty, we stay close to the ground, hoping to move more quickly from one task to the next with "flapping flight."

FLAWED VALUES PRODUCE FLAPPING FLIGHT

The myths we looked at earlier remind us of the subtle way the Enemy "clips our wings" and keeps us grounded. As the retreat participants in that hotel room communicated their frustrations and fears of trying "to become all they could be," I realized they were battling the same problem I still struggle with—twisted convictions that sound like truth when we are not immersed in the Word of God.

Psychiatrist M. Scott Peck gives an analogy that helped me understand the dangers of believing these untruths:

> Our view of reality is like a map. . . . If the map is true and accurate, we will generally know where we are, and if we have decided where we want to go, we will generally know how to get there. If the map is false and inaccurate, we generally will be lost.[2]

Our only hope for having an accurate map is to study the Bible. Knowledge of the truth will strengthen our convictions. Dr. Chris Thurman, in *The Lies We Believe,* says:

> The Bible is God's primary way of giving us the most important truths we need to fight our lies. It's no coincidence that Satan was called the "father of lies." Picture your situation this way: God and Satan are locked in this tremendous struggle for control of your mind. God's weapon is the truth, of course. Satan's is lies. Each day is a battle. Will you play those lie tapes? Or will you listen to the truth? To the degree we choose truth, we'll react appropriately to what happens to us and experience a peace which transcends all understanding. To the degree we choose lies, we will be emotionally and spiritually miserable. When it's a mixture, as it usually is, we live with mixed emotional and spiritual signals.[3]

The lies keep us in bondage and hold us back from being true to ourselves and to God. When we rewrite those lies with biblical truth, instead of "flapping flight," we can choose to soar. Soaring isn't always fun. There's danger and risk—and when you're a beginner, there's more fear than there is later. But there's also exhilaration, freedom, and fulfillment, and a sense of being "carried" by a Power beyond yourself.

EAGLE FLIGHT TRAINING

The story of Esther has always intrigued me. Orphaned. Raised by a relative. Beautiful. Pursued. One year of beauty treatments—special oils, perfumes, and cosmetics—to make a good first impression. Open to wise counsel. Crowned "Queen" Esther by King Xerxes.

What more excitement could a story have? When I was much younger, I envisioned Esther as the "Barbie doll" and King Xerxes as the "Ken doll." I realize the analogy is hard to imagine, but I'm a visual thinker, and it was thrilling to put myself in Barbie's place the day she was "picked" by King

Xerxes (Ken) to be the queen. In my youthful romanticism I wondered how a woman could want to soar any higher than that.

But these were troubled times for the Jews, and their lives were in danger. Word came to Esther from Mordecai: "If you remain silent at this time, relief and deliverance for the Jews will arise from another place, but you and your father's family will perish. And who knows but that you have come to royal position for such a time as this?" (Esther 4:14).

Esther was face-to-face with the biggest risk of her life. God had placed the potential in her to gain an audience with the king. It meant uncertainty, possible failure, and fear. Talk about "eagle" flight training! The rest is history. Because of her obedience and willingness to transcend the fear of failure, her Jewish people were saved from possible annihilation at this frightening time in their history.

IF ONLY I COULD BE AN EAGLE

When I read about women like that, I feel discouraged looking at myself. I have never saved a whole race of people from being wiped out. But I am a woman, and I, like Esther, have a deep desire to be transformed from an ordinary woman into an extraordinary woman who is reaching my potential in all areas.

Several years ago, when my expectations of enjoying teaching junior high students were unfulfilled, I longed to be doing something else. Emotions raged and my *daily choice* was between contentment and dissatisfaction. When my ruling passion was contentment, I was able to choose the action of waiting—with my eyes open!

My biggest battle during this time was to rewrite one of my myths and change it to the truth: "Feeling creative restlessness in my work *does not* mean I'm discontented with God." One of the most helpful activities for me during this time of biblical reprogramming was to honestly and prayerfully answer several questions—first on paper, then face-to-face with a friend.

- What causes most of my frustration, anxiety, and pressure?
- What produces most of my fun, pleasure, and enjoyment?
- Why am I doing the job I'm doing? (If it's only for the money, that's not good enough!)
- What really motivates me?
- What is the most meaningful compliment I've ever received?
- If I could do anything I wanted, without the restrictions of time, money, education, or current responsibilities, what would it be?
- What do I want to be doing ten years from now?
- What do I want on my epitaph?
- What are my greatest strengths?
- What women (currently living) do I admire most?

As I reviewed the answers to those questions, God repeatedly brought to mind the scripture I had selected as my life's verse: "Thou wilt shew me the path of life: in thy presence is fulness of joy; at thy right hand there are pleasures for evermore" (Psalm 16:11, KJV).

The "creative restlessness" in my heart was God's way of preparing me to risk something new. The process of becoming "who I am" is ongoing. Since those early days of struggle in a junior high classroom, it has included motherhood, teaching pregnant girls, becoming a director of Women's Ministries in a local church, being a teacher for an international Bible study organization, launching out into public speaking, and then developing and directing the "Speak Up With Confidence" seminars. Right now my greatest risk is writing. Is this God's next opportunity for me to stretch beyond my comfort zone? What if I fail?

We all have days of "flapping flight" as we struggle to find our customized, God-ordained niche. And just when we think we've found it, He gives us a glimpse of another challenge. Will we stay in "the comfort zone" or will we move into "the risk zone"? More than a few times I have failed, "flapped," and tried again. With each success comes greater confidence. And one day when we spread our wings in the updraft, being lifted by the thermal of His unwavering strength, the whole process will seem normal. Soaring and gliding—that's what we were designed for—not free of risks, not removed from all failure (we still live in this fallen world!), but soaring with a new sense of trust and an inner burst of freedom. To my surprise, I love the adventure!

AN ENCOURAGEMENT

Madeleine L'Engle is a well-known author. Her famous classic *A Wrinkle in Time* has sold millions of copies and touched children and adults everywhere. Al Janssen describes Madeleine's feelings:

> As she wrote, she began to realize that her writing was not just a career. It was a vocation—a calling from God. This story was emerging out of her love for God. It was attempting to reveal his light and love in a fresh way. When she was finished, she knew it was the best writing she'd ever done.[4]

What many people don't know is that for the two and a half years after she wrote that book, more than thirty publishers rejected her manuscript. One day she wrote in her journal, "It's so ironic that I wrote this book for God, and I wrote this book because I finally understand why I'm a writer, and now nobody wants me." She finally gave up hope that the book would be published; yet she was willing to accept herself as a writer, whether she was published or not. It was her calling. She *had* to write. In her journal Madeleine wrote,

> I have to try, but I do not have to succeed. Following Christ has nothing to do with success as the world sees success. It has to do with love. During the ten years when practically nothing I wrote was published, I was as much a writer . . . as I am now; it may happen that

there will come another time when I can't find anyone to publish my work. If this happens, it will matter. It will hurt. But I did learn . . . that success is not my motivation.[5]

Our desire "to be all we can be" is from God. It is not essential that other people validate our success. It's encouraging when they do, but it is not what's ultimately important. When we walk in obedience and fix our minds on truth, our disappointments will eventually produce ruling passions that will result in actions that are honorable and holy. *That's when we soar on wings like eagles!*

PART SIX

THE PASSION
FOR SPIRITUALITY

ELEVEN

WHATEVER THE ABUNDANT LIFE IS, I WANT IT!
To Be a Confident, Growing Christian

What makes life worthwhile is having a big enough objective, something which catches our imagination and lays hold of our allegiance; and this the Christian has, in a way that no other man has. For what higher, more exalted, and more compelling goal can there be than to know God?
J. I. PACKER

Julie was breathless with excitement. The women's retreat had been nothing short of spectacular! The music was perfect—sometimes upbeat, sometimes reflective. And the speakers gave such inspiring messages! Julie had come to know Christ as her personal Savior as a child, but she knew this weekend would be life-changing for her. The time away had been a little touch of Heaven. Now she was headed home, ready to impact her world for Christ!

As Julie's car rounded the corner, she got a glimpse of the house. Home sweet home! She couldn't wait to tell the family about her uplifting experience at the retreat. As she burst into the house, the dog ran smack-dab into her legs, knocking her off balance. Upon impact, Julie's overnight bag flew off in one direction while her Bible landed in the dog dish. At that moment Jennifer, her six-year-old, rushed into the room screaming, "Mom, David's been picking on me and

Dad won't stop him. I hate David and I'm mad at Daddy!"

The television was blaring from the family room and her husband hollered, "Glad you're home, Julie. I'll talk to you after the game's over. Oh, I almost forgot. Your mother called. She's coming for a few days. Said she'd be here for dinner tonight."

Rock music bellowed from David's room upstairs. Still in a prone position after colliding with the dog, Julie surveyed the remnants of her kitchen. Dishes were piled high in the sink and randomly placed all over the countertop. A trail of popcorn ran from the microwave oven to the television set. Pop bottles and candy wrappers were here and there. Lifting herself from the floor, she stood up and tried to take a step. Her feet were mobile, but her shoes weren't. Pancake syrup had glued them to the floor.

With blood pressure rising, Julie stomped down the hall, crushing every kernel of popcorn in her path. Finally arriving at the throne of King Couch Potato, she sucked in air, took careful aim, and fired: "I am mad. No, I'm not mad. *I'm furious! I leave for one weekend—just one weekend—and this place turns into a garbage dump!* There's garbage in the kitchen. Garbage on the floor. Garbage sports on the television. Garbage music on the radio in your son's room. And Jennifer has had no supervision. This place could not be in worse shape if I'd left the dog in charge! And you call yourself a father?"

Bull's eye! Her ammunition was gone, but Julie knew she hit her mark. Pivoting on her heel, she stiffened and marched out of the room like a trained soldier leaving the battlefield. Enemy wounded. Mission accomplished.

Now back in the kitchen, she picked up her overnight bag and then reached for her Bible. Wiping dog food off the gilded edges, she started to crumble. There was a knot in her throat. The tough lady was beginning to fight back tears. The in-charge, always-under-control, Mrs. I-Am-All-Together was falling apart.

Pondering the "life-changing" commitment she made on the weekend, Julie voiced her question out loud: "God, where are You now? Is it possible for a woman to experience true spirituality in the real world? How can I be a confident, growing Christian with a family like mine? Every time I think I have it together, I don't. Every time I get spiritually inspired, my life falls apart. My emotions are exploding. I'm worried about my kids. I don't understand my husband. My faith in God is like a roller coaster. When I'm at the top, I can conquer the world and Jesus is wonderful. When I'm at the bottom, I feel like giving up. God has let me down. And then I feel guilty because good Christians don't think things like that. Why doesn't somebody write a for-real book called, Dog Dish Christianity: How to Live the Abundant Life with a Rotten Husband and Crummy Kids?"

"READY? AIM! FIRE!"

What really happens to us when we have days like Julie experienced? Married or single, we all have circumstances, events, and people who shoot holes in our spiritual balloon. When the helium is fresh, the balloon reaches ever upward, cavorting with the wind, resisting the downward tug of the string, bouncing back up to full grandeur with every playful pull.

But within a short time, the gas that pumped it up begins to escape. The balloon loses some of its elasticity and begins its downward spiral, sometimes lingering, wistfully trying to imitate its former status, but falling far short of the goal. Suddenly it's Monday morning. And the exhilarating retreat weekend has now been replaced by the daily grind. Does Christianity work without a background of inspirational music and motivational speakers?

THE PASSION FOR SPIRITUALITY

The abundant Christian life. I want it. You want it. Some people seem to have it. But *how* do we get it? Remember the verse that says, "I am come that they might have life, and that they might have it more abundantly" (John 10:10, KJV)? Evidently there *is* a way to get it, and that's *why* Jesus came in the first place, but probably the people who experience the "abundant" Christian life have husbands and kids that are more spiritual than ours. Or maybe single women are the only ones who get to experience Christianity at its best. Wrong!

The phrase, *abundant Christian life,* seems to indicate there's a way to live out our spirituality with confidence, fruitfulness, and increasing maturity. Francis Schaeffer wrote a book called *True Spirituality,* and in it he says, "The question before us is *what the Christian life*—true spirituality—*really is, and how it may be lived in a twentieth-century setting.*"[1] That sure *is* the question, and his book outlines several helpful biblical principles for living the authentic, abundant Christian life.

But with all due respect for the countless numbers of theologians who've written on this topic, I still need help with knowing how all the rhetoric applies to the real world. With an IQ like mine (something less than genius level!), I need somebody to spell it out. *How* can I live the Christian life abundantly in the framework of my daily life?

BLUEPRINT OF THE WAR ZONE

As we take a look back at Julie's situation, we may gain some insights that will help us.

Julie's Expectation: After her uplifting spiritual retreat weekend, Julie was bursting with enthusiasm for the Lord. She *had* to tell her precious family about the messages, the music, and the new closeness she experienced in her walk with God. Her expectations were threefold:

1. She wanted the family to vicariously experience the spiritual mountaintop of the weekend.
2. She expected her husband to get his heart right with God and become the spiritual leader of the home after he listened to the cassette tape of the female speaker she had just heard at the retreat. Even though she knew that he didn't like "women preachers," she was sure that this woman's mes-

sage would "nail" him and he would come back
to God.
3. She anticipated coming home to a clean, well-run
household with a happy husband and children. She
envisioned Jennifer and David participating in
games and outdoor activities with their father, enjoying the closeness of family ties and cherishing time
alone with Dad.

Julie's Disappointment: Her devastation was so obvious we almost don't need to comment on it. The family did not
care at all about reviewing *her* spiritual high. The *last* thing
her husband wanted to listen to was "that lady preacher's
tape," nor was his heart any closer to coming back to the
Lord. And as for the house, we've already said enough! And
how about the close family time? Talk about disappointments!
She had them!

Julie's Longing: At best, Julie's deepest desire was for
a little hunk of Eden in her own backyard. She wanted her
marriage and family life to be the way God intended it before
sin corrupted the human race. With her own heart touched
supernaturally on the weekend, she believed God could, and
that He *would* touch those in her family, too. She longed for a
family that lived out the principles of the abundant Christian
life. With an honest heart, she knew her goal was to be a
confident, growing Christian, and she wanted the same for
her husband and children. If Julie couldn't have that, she at
least felt she deserved a clean home and a civil family. Disappointment "lowered the boom," and Julie's longing produced
flat-out rage!

Julie's Emotion: To say that Julie "blew a gasket" would
be an understatement. It was as if she shook up a bottle of
soda pop, positioned it in front of her husband, and "pulled the
cork!" Julie's emotional outburst even surprised *her*! She got
so involved in her "garbage" speech that she worked in a line
from previous disappointments as she referred to his "garbage
sports on television."

Julie's Decision: Julie had just experienced a dynamic,

encouraging conference centered on biblical principles for victorious Christian living. At first glance it would appear that her values system could not have been any stronger than it was after the uplifting weekend retreat. The problem for Julie was that she lived her Christian life from one "high" to the next. She seldom opened her Bible in between Sundays. The mainstays of her prayer life consisted of asking God to bless the food and begging Him to get through to her unspiritual husband and son.

In spite of her emotionally charged decision made at the retreat to "set her world on fire for Jesus," she still had damaged convictions due to her misconceptions about the Christian life and her lack of time in the Word of God. If Julie's values system had been based on truth, instead of misconceptions, she could have made a godly decision, with or without the emotional high of the women's retreat.

Julie's Drive/Passion: Sifting her strong emotions through a false set of values, she chose ruling passions of resentment and anger.

Julie's Action: With resentment still steaming, her twisted actions varied from screaming to silence. First, the anger was directed toward her husband for being so lethargic and uninvolved with the children. One of her favorite actions was to play her cassette tapes of Christian messages and music loudly when he was home. She wanted to let him know he was *not* the spiritual leader she wanted him to be and he should feel guilty about it. Her anger also had a ripple effect on the children as they got caught in the wake of their parents' war zone.

Finally, the anger was directed toward God—subliminally at first, then blatantly. After all, the God of creation, Mighty Worker of miracles, *could* get through to her husband if He wanted to. Couldn't He? Then why didn't He? If Julie's values had been biblical, she could have lived her life by the principle we read in 1 Peter 3:1-2: "Wives, in the same way be submissive to your husbands so that, if any of them do not believe the word, they may be won over without words by the behavior of their wives, when they see the purity and reverence of your lives."

IDENTIFYING THE BATTLEGROUND

Julie's unfulfilled expectations brought about deep disappointment. In her heart, she longed to be a growing Christian, confident in her walk with God. Instead, she felt like a spiritual zero, aimlessly looking for a quick-fix solution and wondering what to do next. The flaws in her values produced confusion, and the confusion made her question her own faith.

It happens to all of us at one time or another. A missionary writes about the fruit of faulty foundations:

> Our inability to develop a truly God-shaped set of expectations easily could leave us wandering out the forty years or so of our adult lives in our own self-made desert wilderness. In my case, the greatest consequence of long-term, misplaced expectations has been their deadening effect on spiritual vitality. I questioned God, myself, my circumstances. . . . *God must not love me the way He loves others,* I thought. *I must be on Jesus' blacklist. I guess I'm just one of those Christians that God can't use.*[2]

Our greatest battles most often come when we get caught up in the comparison game. Most of us right now could name somebody we think "has it together" spiritually. And what's her profile?

She looks good. She sounds good. She smells good. And her baby never spits up on anyone. This woman's children don't talk out loud during church services. Her cat uses the litter box. She is a wonderful Bible teacher, and she knows all the appropriate scripture verses (from memory) for everybody's need. She's always smiling and never yells. This woman has never had a run in her stockings. Her husband is a spiritual giant, and when she teaches Bible study she always makes reference to his strong Christian leadership in their home. She leads such a "blessed" life, it appears that God loves her more than He loves you.

We hate her. (We know we shouldn't use that word about a "dear" Christian sister, but it is our honest emotional response.)

If I pause long enough to think rationally, I know the battleground is my own mind. I have a *powerful* ability to visualize what isn't real. The dictionary defines *imagination* as "the act or power of forming a mental image of something not present to the senses or never before wholly perceived in reality." When I think about how "spiritually perfect" someone else's life is, my imagination always makes her life *better* than it is and it makes my life *worse* than it really is. In my mind, she is "dripping" with the fruits of the Spirit, and I can't even find a blossom on my fruit tree!

As I create untrue mental images, the Enemy attacks with vengeance. Satan has had years to observe me, and he knows me better than I know myself. He has already determined my point of vulnerability—the mind! Ephesians 6:12 confirms that there's a war raging: "For our struggle is not against flesh and blood, but against the rulers, against the authorities, against the powers of this dark world and against the spiritual forces of evil in heavenly realms."

Is there any hope of defeating the "Father of Lies"?

RECOGNIZING MISCONCEPTIONS

In our quest to establish healthy values, we need to stop long enough to analyze our thinking. Why do we act and react the way we do? Is it an automatic response, based on the people, events, and circumstances in our lives? Or is Satan so powerful that we end up being pawns in his hand, controlled at his whim? If so, we will always have an excuse for our lack of spiritual maturity. We can slap a surprised look on our faces when our actions are misguided and say, "I'm so sorry. The Devil made me do it!"

When we own up to the truth, we realize *we choose our own ruling passions,* based on the state of our minds at the time of decision making. Second Corinthians 10:5 (KJV) says, "Casting down imaginations, and every high thing that exalteth itself against the knowledge of God, and bringing into captivity every thought to the obedience of Christ."

My ungodly imaginations produce misconceptions about

the Christian life. I don't like to admit it, because I'm made responsible to God for replacing my thoughts with biblical truth that will produce sound values. I would prefer to have Him supernaturally "zap" me with right thinking. Instead, He's given me His Word as a guidebook. Void of excuses for blaming other people and events for "doing me in," I must face the truth: If my convictions are based on unbiblical misconceptions, it's my fault when I act and react with ungodly responses.

In the opening story, Julie's misconceptions were typical of the flawed values of all of us who've failed at being confident, growing Christians. Add to that our response to "Mrs. Perfect and her Happy Christian Family," and it's easy to itemize the list of misconceptions that subtly get ingrained in our values.

- God can't use me unless I'm a spiritual giant.
- If I work hard, God will give me spiritual fruit in my ministry.
- It's my Christian duty to be perfect.
- Visible results are the measuring stick of spiritual effectiveness.
- I could do more for God if my family were perfect and if I were more talented.
- Speaking and teaching are the most important spiritual gifts.
- The abundant Christian life is always filled with adrenalin-producing highs.
- I would be a better Christian if my husband loved Jesus more. (We can substitute "mother, sister, brother, or friend" for the word *husband.*)

Rusty Rustenbach, the missionary I quoted earlier on page 185, goes on to say:

A deeper investigation of my (faulty foundations) caused me to see that they were inventions of my evangelical subculture rather than sound biblical beliefs. Although at times God gives struggle-free periods of growth, consistent fruit for my labor, and a path free from problems, it may be less than biblical to expect Him to work this way all the time. Scripture presents a different view-point, one we naturally resist: *reality*.[3]

REALITY STRATEGY

For me, facing reality starts with comparing my misconceptions with what the Bible actually says. I've always claimed for myself that inspiring passage from Jeremiah 17:7-8:

> Blessed is the man who trusts in the LORD, whose confidence is in him. He will be like a tree planted by the water that sends out its roots by the stream. It does not fear when heat comes; its leaves are always green. It has no worries in a year of drought and never fails to bear fruit.

On first glance it appears that if I work hard for God, I will always bear spiritual fruit. Wrong! Working hard is *not* what it takes to be a fruitful Christian.

My whole personality rebels against that fact! I *love* to work and be rewarded for it. On those fancy psychological tests, my profile comes out as the person who likes work before play. I like to know what God's "to do" list has on it for me each day. Then I like to perform with excellence (faithfully checking off each item on my list as I come to it), and at the end of the day I'd like to be rewarded with the prize fruit mentioned in Galatians 5:22: "love, joy, peace, patience, kindness, goodness, faithfulness, gentleness and self-control."

The unbiblical view that hard work always results in spiritual fruit leaves no room for God-ordained interruptions, health problems, waiting rooms, or people who think or speak more slowly than I do. And the very nature of patience (idling your motor when you feel like stripping your gears) is *flexibility* instead of *rigidity*.

Last week I met with a group of Christian professional women, and when a psychologist looked at my scores on a test we had taken, she said, "Do you know you have the most *intense* personality type there is?" (No surprise there!) My unbendable work ethic turns me into a screaming wife and mother (like Julie) one minute and a basket case of tears the next. How can I ever be a fruitful Christian by biblical standards when I'm trapped in this "structured" mindset?

My *expectation* is to be a woman who trusts in the Lord and brings glory to Him. The *disappointment* comes when my rigid work ethic doesn't bring the fulfillment of true spirituality. My *longing* is to experience the fruit of the Spirit by reacting to life's events (including the surprises) with love, joy, peace, patience, kindness, goodness, faithfulness, gentleness, and self-control.

When that doesn't happen, my *emotions* take over, and I try "to organize this place or person or project (whatever is in my path) into shape!" If I'm working with a non-family member, my emotions are like water behind a dam—at times turbulent and powerful, but with the outward "appearance of control." If I'm with family or close friends, the dam breaks, flooding the person with negative criticism and undeserved verbal attacks.

My *decision* involves running those emotions through my belief system. Accepting the misconception, "If I work hard, God will give me spiritual fruit in my ministry," I decide on a *ruling passion* of zealous workaholism. And my resulting *action* is to control everything and everybody in my path, manipulating them into doing (my opinion of) God's will. And in my heart I think I'm doing something good for God and them. But I'm not.

"Reality strategy" means taking a closer look at *the tree planted by the water*. It must be important because the Bible refers to it in Psalm 1:3-4 as well as in Jeremiah 17:7-8. Since God doesn't waste words, He must have wanted us to capture the essence of this "tree theology."

When our firm belief, assurance, and trust are in Him, we are "like a tree . . . that sends out its roots by the stream." Instead of experiencing outward anxiety and attitudes of workaholism, perfectionism, and manipulation of others, we spend time establishing the inside root system. We do this through prayer, Bible study, discipline, listening without talking, meditating, memorizing His Word, evaluating our motives before organizing activities—*being* rather than *doing*. The reward is not applause from an audience. No standing ovations here. The quiet results are two-fold: *invisible* (no fear when the "heat" is on) and *visible* ("green leaves in drought time").

A spiritual renewal. I need to experience this. No music. No speakers. Just Him and me. I think I'm hungry for it. But I'm afraid of it. I'm more used to noise. Silence frightens me. It means having to face my true motives, revealing my hidden heartbeat. It means owning up to my *real* reasons for working so hard and admitting I'm a beginner at prayer even though I've known Him personally for years. It means reading His Word because I long to hear from Him rather than to mark my progress on the "Read Through the Bible in a Year" chart. It means discovering my true "hidden agenda" and dumping my calendar and "lists" for a block of time with no telephone, no radio, no television, no outside interference, no speeches, no deadlines.

I wonder. What was it like for Moses to enter the Tent of Meeting? It must have been humbling and spectacular, for "The LORD would speak to Moses face to face, as a man speaks with his friend" (Exodus 33:11). I'm really wondering what He wants to say to me—if only I'd give Him a chance.

PROFILE OF A COMMITTED SOLDIER

Apart from Christ, nowhere in Scripture do we see a more passionate man than Paul. I'm sure he could identify with workaholics. Before his conversion, he persecuted the saints with full gusto. After his Damascus Road experience, he used that same intense drive to serve His God with equal zeal.

On his second missionary journey he and Silas had several "waits" before they were led by the Spirit—in a very roundabout way—to go to Philippi. (I like the direct route myself, and I have a feeling Paul felt the same way.) I wonder what his *expectations* were. A city-wide evangelistic crusade? Media coverage? A soul-winning seminar for local pastors? An autograph party at the local Christian bookstore? (Oops! I guess his books weren't off the press yet.)

We would no doubt be safe in assuming there were some *disappointments* upon arrival. Instead of an impressive crowd to share with, they met with a handful of women by a river and shared their faith. One responded. Then a slave girl followed them. Paul cast a demon out of her in Jesus' name, thus destroying the earning potential of the girl's owners. The rest is history. Paul and Silas were jailed, stripped, severely beaten, with their feet fastened in stocks.

If I had been there, my deepest longing would have been to escape and leave! Not Paul. His *longing* was a deep yearning to preach the gospel and to lead people to Jesus Christ. Paul's *emotion,* when defined as an initial automatic response, is unclear. There is nothing in Acts 16 that would lead us to believe he was upset by this outrageous treatment. Paul's *decision-making process* was so rooted in a God-honoring foundation that his *ruling passion* of choosing joy in spite of suffering was almost automatic.

He practiced the presence of Christ. Thus, his *action* of praying and singing hymns to God in the middle of his imprisonment led to another holy action. Instead of escaping after the earthquake, he stayed and led the jailer to Christ. R. C. Sproul vividly describes this remarkable man:

> He was clearly a man of great passion, a man marked
> by impulsive zeal even before his conversion. The Holy
> Spirit never squelched that passion but rather har-
> nessed it and redirected it to the benefit of the Kingdom
> of God. He was a man of many tears, weeping with
> tenderness with those who suffered. His pen was made
> lyrical by the impulse of his own deep emotion. . . .
> His personality was a kaleidoscope of vignettes of pas-
> sion—flashing here with intellectual brilliance and there
> with the warmth of compassion.[4]

It was Paul who gave this challenge: "Endure hardship with us like a good soldier of Christ Jesus. No one serving as a soldier gets involved in civilian affairs—he wants to please his commanding officer" (2 Timothy 2:3-4).

FRUITFUL LIVING IN THE REAL WORLD

Paul inspires me. But unlike him, I *do* have a few civilian duties that need to be taken care of every day. He wasn't married. I am. He didn't have a child. I do. But what can I learn from this man that will help me live out true spirituality in the twentieth century?

He practiced the "automatic response syndrome." Paul had a mindset that anticipated disappointments beforehand. It was no surprise to him that his demonstrative faith produced negative responses from godless people. It was the natural result of living in a fallen world.

His longing was already firmly established. His goal in life was to go and make disciples. His values were so firmly established in truth—God's truth—that he often "automatically" skipped a negative emotional reaction when circumstances, people, and events didn't go his way. His ruling passion was an intense love for God and his actions were a demonstration of holy zeal.

"MESS HALL" THEOLOGY

There are days when my "marching boots" are stuck in pancake syrup. My patience is thin. My love is conditional. My joy has evaporated. Peace and self-control have passed me by. On those days I need to clearly identify—by faith, not by feeling—what were my disappointments that produced my longing for change. Instead of "flying by my emotions," blaming the Devil or other people for my twisted actions, *I must be a responsible soldier.*

My orders are already in print. The Commander deserves my allegiance. My values system must be checked and rechecked for misconceptions that produce ungodly ruling passions. To be completely honest is difficult. I'm tempted to go back to old patterns. I secretly like working hard for God's approval and practicing my "list mentality." But growth takes time. He knows that. I know that. And to my surprise, His abundance is mine *in* the process—not as a prize at the end of my tour of duty.

TWELVE

ME—GOD'S WOMAN?
To Live Out My Reason for Being

*There is no magic in small plans. When I consider
my ministry, I think of the world. Anything less than
that would not be worthy of Christ nor His will
for my life.*
HENRIETTA MEARS

The above statement motivates me! It's passionate. Challenging. It's spiritually inspiring. It lets me know there are some women who have led the way when it comes to dynamic commitment and personal sacrifice.

Henrietta Mears was a Sunday school teacher who wrote lessons for her students. Her faithfulness in small things led to the founding of Gospel Light Publications. Dr. Bill Bright, founder of Campus Crusade for Christ, points to her as one of the key spiritual influences in his life. As a prayer warrior, she was a tremendous encouragement to world-renowned evangelist Billy Graham and many others. One woman with "a reason for *being.*"

Then there was Corrie ten Boom, dedicated servant of Christ. I heard her speak to a packed auditorium on three different occasions. She said, "I have learned in my years on earth to hold everything loosely, because when I hold things tightly, God has to pry my fingers away. And that hurts. That hurts." Corrie had learned the secret—the essence of true spirituality. What is it? Relinquishment, plain and simple.

> There was never a doubt in Corrie's mind about the work God called her to. This commission was to bear the Good News of God's love, His forgiveness and His faithfulness to the whole world. One would think that when released from Ravensbruck (prison camp) in February, 1945, she would want to go home—to a place of safety, security, peace and rest, surrounded by friends who would minister to her. She *deserved* that. But that thought couldn't have been further from Corrie's mind because she lived under divine constraint. She believed God commissioned her for a work.[1]

And *work* she did! In her travels around the world to convey a powerful message that burned within her, Corrie often quoted the last verse of her favorite hymn, *When I Survey the Wondrous Cross:*

> Were the whole realm of nature mine,
> That were a present far too small:
> Love so amazing, so divine,
> Demands my soul, my life, my all.

Each time I heard Corrie speak, there was a holy stirring in my soul. The message of this woman was so convicting and strong I was often moved to tears. And she didn't fit the pattern for most successful public speakers. She was overweight. Plain. Old-fashioned hair net holding gray tresses in place. Broken English. Common, homemade visual aids. No dynamic delivery techniques. So what was this woman's secret?

Corrie's secret was *a passion for God that resulted in relinquishment of her personal rights,* which included all her expectations that He should lead her along an easy path.

J. Oswald Sanders defines what we're talking about: "Spirituality is not easy to define, but its presence or absence can easily be discerned. . . . It is the power to change the atmosphere by one's presence, the unconscious influence that makes Christ and spiritual things real to others."[2]

Corrie's *disappointments* must have been overwhelming. Internment camp. The death of precious family members. Inhumane living conditions. Surrounded by hateful, cruel soldiers. Lice. Disease. Pain and suffering. Surely she must have *longed* for life as it was before the war. Certainly for Corrie and her family, life was not fair.

Had I been in her place, how would I have responded? My *longing* would very likely have been to escape cruelty and attempt survival by forgetting the atrocities of the war and burying myself in personal comforts and a safe haven. My *emotions* would have been evident in angry outbursts against my captors and in a negative, critical attitude toward the God who allowed me to experience such brutality.

Anyone with a flawed belief system would have immediately gone through the *decision-making process,* arriving at an instant *ruling passion* of anger toward God. My *action* would likely have been withdrawal and isolation. Anything to forget the pain. Every lonely day would have been another opportunity for anger to breed resentment and hate in my heart toward those unfeeling people and "the God who wasn't there when I needed Him."

But not Corrie! She had *a reason for being* that went far beyond life as we know it. For her, life itself was a mission from God. Her eternal mindset was so firmly established that she looked at time here on earth as a fleeting, short prelude to eternity. I could hear her life resounding with an echo of the psalmist's words, "My times are in your hands" (Psalm 31:15). Pain, suffering, even brutal existence at Ravensbruck were all a stage upon which His power could be viewed by others. God had given her a unique and special task. A high calling. He was worthy of nothing less than her all.

THE POWER OF DISAPPOINTMENT

The secret of experiencing true spirituality seems ultimately tied to how we handle our unfulfilled expectations. Do we hold our disappointments closely, fondling our hurts, ruminating over the injustices we've experienced and the unkind, unfeeling, or cruel treatment of others? That response breeds self-pity, discouragement, depression, and ultimately despair. Sometimes despair leads to suicide, and that pleases the "Father of Lies." By nursing our disappointments, we open ourselves to satanic attack.

I believe that the greatest single cause of spiritual defeat is the Enemy's ability to get us preoccupied with our disappointments—especially personal disappointment in ourselves. We sin. We have a guilty conscience. We confess our sin. But our memory of past spiritual failure fills our visual image of "who we are." We try to work hard to please God, hoping to somehow offset the "badness" of our "real" selves—but we fail. Now we feel guilty. We expected to feel better. But we don't. And our disappointment leads to discouragement. So we sin again . . . and again. We've experienced the same cycle repeatedly. We feel powerless to change.

DEALING WITH GUILT

I think David understood the pain of disappointment. I think he struggled with guilt. I'm sure he felt like a spiritual failure. After he committed adultery with Bathsheba and then saw to it that her husband, Uriah, was killed in the front lines of battle, he must have gone through an overwhelming inner struggle.

David's Expectation: He was selected above all the rest to be the king. He was "the man after God's own heart." Surely he would have expected joy, success, honor, fulfillment, and spiritual victory in his life. (I've never been a queen or even close to royalty, but I can identify with being spiritually high and feeling invincible—and expecting that feeling to last forever.)

David's Disappointment: I can only imagine the degree of David's disappointment in himself when the reality of his sin caught up with him. When confronted by the prophet Nathan, David was a broken man. Although his prayer in Psalm

51 reveals the *action* of confession following his wicked deeds, we can trace the chain reaction as he bares his soul to God:

> Have mercy on me, O God, according to your unfailing love; according to your great compassion blot out my transgressions. Wash away all my iniquity and cleanse me from my sin. For I know my transgressions, and my sin is always before me. (Psalm 51:1-3)

It's pretty obvious that David was feeling heavy guilt. He had blown it. His previous actions were so bad he probably would have been kicked out of my church. He might never have served in Christian leadership again in my town. He was a marked man. Adultery. Cover-up. Murder. Scandal.

David's Emotions: Initially, his feelings must have been full of *immoral lust.*

> From the roof he saw a woman bathing. The woman was very beautiful, and David sent someone to find out about her. . . . Then David sent messengers to get her. She came to him, and he slept with her. (2 Samuel 11:2-4)

Later his emotions must have swung to *fear* of being found out and then to *guilt* for having committed adultery and murdering Uriah.

David's Longing: It's hard to identify David's real longing in Scripture, because he's so busy covering his tracks. Then the answer becomes obvious. His longing was for "life as it was before this major headache." His personal integrity was shot to pieces. His first son by Bathsheba died. His relationship with God was distant. Nathan the prophet was "on his case." And no matter how hard he tried to cover up his sin, it wouldn't work. (My life doesn't parallel with David's on all counts, but I do know the deep longing to "fix" my problems myself. When we long for peace in the middle of chaos, we often tend to say, "I'll do it myself, God.")

David's Decision: In his prayer, we see David's open

admission of the results that stemmed from his flawed belief system. He continues his confession with these words:

> Against you, you only, have I sinned and done what is evil in your sight. . . . Surely you desire truth in the inner parts; you teach me wisdom in the inmost place. (Psalm 51:4,6)

TRUTH IN THE INNER PARTS

And here lies the central message of this entire book. If we are ever going to experience true spirituality, we must develop a biblical belief system that will form the foundation for unshakable convictions and provide the framework for ruling passions that honor God—no matter what disappointments we experience.

I wonder what David's myths were. He might have thought:

- "I am king and I deserve it all. A little personal gratification is appropriate in my position."
- "It's easier to cover up my problems than to face them."
- "I know I'm God's chosen man, so my spiritual relationship doesn't need much maintenance."

Am I being too hard on David? I don't think so. We all struggle with misconceptions that *feel* like truth. Dr. Frank Minirth says,

> Do we actually believe lies? We certainly do! On an intellectual and, most certainly, on an emotional level, we all wrestle with lies; and our response to them may very well determine our happiness or sadness, peace or worry, and mental health or mental disorders.[3]

I'd like to add that those lies determine our ruling passions and destroy our spiritual health.

So *how* do we develop truth in "the inner parts"? Solomon gives us the answer:

> If you accept my words and store up my commands
> within you, turning your ear to wisdom and applying
> your heart to understanding, and if you call out for in-
> sight and cry aloud for understanding, and if you look
> for it as for silver and search for it as for hidden treas-
> ure, then you will understand the fear of the LORD and
> find the knowledge of God. (Proverbs 2:1-5)

One of the functions of the Holy Spirit that I value most is His ability to give me a sense of "uneasiness" when I'm in a decision-making situation, operating with a flawed belief system. In the heat of emotion, we normally don't stop long enough to ask, "What are my firm convictions on this subject that will help to give me direction as I decide on a ruling passion and then on an action?" We're too busy reacting and throwing a royal fit because life isn't turning out the way we'd hoped it would.

So we automatically select an ungodly ruling passion and blame the resulting devastation on the rotten people in our lives, the "stupid" circumstance, or the Devil. Satan *is* power-ful—very powerful—but I don't think we should blame him for *everything*.

For me, the process of "developing truth in the inner parts" begins with an acknowledgement of the Bible as the source of truth. My follow-up action must be a choice to store up His words and commands in my heart by reading and memorizing Scripture on a regular basis. (It's not easy. And it takes more discipline than I'd like to admit.) Then, when disappointments come—and they *always* do—I must stop long enough to evalu-ate my reaction. During that brief interlude, the Holy Spirit has an opportunity to reveal truth to me.

Because of my "humanness," that pause may come *after* my emotional outburst. It's a temptation to feel so defeated after an emotional explosion that we go back to the guilt syn-drome. We think, "I've already blown it, so it doesn't really matter what my actions are." That's a lie! We need to explore *why* the emotional reaction was so strong.

If I do wait, *before* instantly choosing a negative ruling

passion, I can sift my emotions through my convictions. The pause here gives the Holy Spirit a chance to bring that sense of "uneasiness" if I'm starting to base a ruling passion on a myth. I'm beginning to appreciate that feeling. But it's hard. It's admitting I don't have all the answers. It's acknowledging that my personal spiritual journey is still very much in process. It's sacrificing ego for integrity.

The Holy Spirit becomes my teacher and guide, and responding to His leading becomes an exciting adventure. The more I take in the wisdom of God, the more accurate my belief system is and the more often my ruling passions result in honorable and holy actions.

David's Drive/Passion: Without a doubt, David made many wrong choices in his life. But after an intense struggle, David's ruling passion was his love for God.

David's Action: His action is played out in the biblical record. He chose repentance, and that resulted in a restored relationship with God and a dynamic future ministry. His prayer to His God during this time has always touched an inner chord with me:

> Cleanse me with hyssop, and I will be clean; wash me,
> and I will be whiter than snow. Create in me a pure
> heart, O God, and renew a steadfast spirit within me.
> Do not cast me from your presence or take your Holy
> Spirit from me. Restore to me the joy of your salvation.
> (Psalm 51:7,10-12)

There is an overwhelming joy that accompanies confession, repentance, and the restoration of close relationships with God and people we were alienated from due to our own negative ruling passions. It's humbling. Pride is put aside. Masks are removed. Honesty replaces falsehood. That which was hidden is revealed. Without confession and repentance, restoration does not occur.

But the alternative is like a cancer that attacks the body's lymph system. You never know where the next tumor will show up. You can cover the disease up for a while, but before long it always becomes visible again. The cover-up is never worth its reward. David's a perfect example of this.

RELINQUISHING OUR EXPECTATIONS
AND DISAPPOINTMENTS

For the Christian woman, life needs to be a process of relinquishing our unrealistic expectations. It's especially hard for dreamers like me. (What's my favorite luncheon date? Spending a couple of hours with a creative, intelligent Christian who believes that God can do the impossible. I love brainstorming with people like that!)

But when we dream big, disappointments fall hard. We expect too much from people and projects. And everything in us wants to hold on to our disappointments. Our personal monologue goes something like this:

- "I *believed* something would happen, and it didn't."
- "I *expected* intimacy in a friendship, and it was withheld."
- "I *knew* my marriage would be permanent, but I'm divorced."
- "I *anticipated* success in a job, and I failed."
- "I *assumed* I'd have healthy self-worth by now, but I don't."
- "I'm *convinced* God forgives sin, but I feel guilty."
- "I *thought* serving Jesus would be easy, and it's hard."

Our list could go on and on. What we expect falls short of what we experience. What we hope for in a relationship, circumstance, or event doesn't always work out. There is a gap between what we believe will take place and what actually happens. Disappointment sets in.

The essence of relinquishment is "releasing our grasp." It's giving up our rights. Surrendering our plan. Letting go. It is the hardest task of all. It goes against our natural instinct.

Our disappointments in life provide an ongoing opportunity to release our private hurts and painful memories to Him.

The relinquishment of our unfulfilled expectations has the surprising potential of freeing us to experience greater intimacy with God. It's an act of trusting Him when we cannot see a positive outcome. Relinquishment puts a stop to our manipulation of other people and releases the Holy Spirit to do the supernatural through the power of prayer. Relinquishment starves little resentments that have the potential to grow into roots of bitterness.

As I was writing this week, the mailman came. Opening a magazine, an article caught my eye—"The Bittersweet of Letting Go." Ruth Senter shares her thoughts on this same topic:

> Sometimes relinquishment means giving up a cherished dream, a plan, an illusion. Life is often a series of adjustments—fitting our dreams to reality. I have my notions of what life should be. Unfortunately, my notions are sometimes more typical of paradise than of the cracked utopia in which I live. For some of us, relinquishment comes when we surrender our fantasies. I may never shake the world with great accomplishments by the time I'm 50 years old. Not every day will be peaceful. Not everyone will love me. People will make mistakes or disappoint me. Goals may rot on my journal page. Projections fall far short.[4]

But where do we go with our disappointments? Is there a ritual we can go through that will somehow make it easier? I'm afraid this whole idea of relinquishment requires more than I'm willing to give. I have to lay my "cherished" disappointments at the foot of Calvary and *not* pick them up again!

THE SUPREME EXAMPLE

What was it like for the Son of God to experience the ultimate disappointment? The only man in history to be born without sin was asked by His Father to pay the penalty for all of mankind.

He had experience with handling the disappointments of others. When people followed Him because they expected to get free bread, He exposed their wrong motives. When they expected to crown Him king, He quietly disappeared from among them.

Then it happened. He had that final meal with the Twelve. All that talk about the coming of the Comforter, about the vine and branches, and about how they should love each other, they didn't understand. He was so serious. He talked about leaving, but He spoke with expectant hope about coming back. Why, if He was coming back, did He give this long speech at the dinner table that night?

It was time to go. He took his intimate friends—Peter, James, and John. He would need them to pray there at the Mount of Olives. Surely He could count on them. Out of His sad awareness of what the next day held, Jesus bared His heart to His best friends: "My soul is overwhelmed with sorrow to the point of death," He said (Matthew 26:38). But when He returned, they were sleeping. It happened three times in a row.

Withdrawing from them, He fell to the ground and prayed, "My Father, if it is possible, may this cup be taken from me" (Matthew 26:39).

I can almost hear Him pleading, "Father, is there *any* other way than the cross?" *At that moment in time, did Jesus have an expectation that just maybe He wouldn't have to face the crucifixion?*

Then, almost instantaneously, He relinquished His own rights, and we hear Him say, "Yet not as I will, but as you will" (Matthew 26:39).

For Jesus, the decision was immediate. He knew His mission—a special task for which He alone was chosen. His longing was to please the Father. His convictions were set in truth. Surrendering His rights, He relinquished any hold on the thought that there might be another alternative that would make it possible for you and me to experience forgiveness of sin and intimacy with God. There was no other way. With a ruling passion of love, His action of "obedience unto death—even death on a cross" cemented for all time His *reason for being.*

LIVING OUT MY REASON FOR BEING

I'm not Corrie ten Boom. I'm just a regular kind of woman trying to be a "for-real" Christian in twentieth-century America. I remember wondering if God talked to Corrie out loud. She seemed to hear Him so clearly. I long for that.

If we could talk face-to-face, I wonder what He'd say to me. Right now, in the middle of my ordinary days, am I accomplishing His purpose for my life? Am I living out His reason for creating me? Do I have *a passion for God*?

I wonder if I'm getting any closer to *true spirituality* than I was last year. With all my heart, I don't want to be an ordinary Christian. He deserves more. I chuckle at that lofty thought. My fingers are in peanut butter and my phone is ringing and someone is at the door. But then I remember. God has always used ordinary people to carry out His extraordinary mission.

J. Oswald Sanders was right. True spirituality is the power to change the atmosphere by our presence. It's *the unconscious influence* that makes Christ and spiritual things real to others. That must mean that *being fully woman and fully God's* can, over time, become as natural as breathing.

True spirituality means relinquishing our expectations and disappointments to Him. It's being "like a tree planted by the water"—and sinking deep roots. The psalmist reminds us that God "satisfies the thirsty and fills the hungry with good things" (Psalm 107:9).

> Lord, be glorified in me. Let Your supernatural presence be felt by the people in my life. Free me from false guilt. Establish my heart in truth. Help me to encourage others on their journey home. Give me the boldness to speak and the wisdom to be quiet. Let Your creativity flow through me. But center my lofty thoughts on You. Teach me the value of solitude. Slow me down. Quiet my heart. Give me an eternal mindset. Purify my motives. Keep me from demanding seeable results. Teach me to pray. Guard my convictions. Let my ruling passion be my love for You.

NOTES

CHAPTER 1: HIDDEN LONGINGS OF THE HEART

1. *Webster's New World Dictionary of the American Language,* David B. Guralnik ed. (Nashville: The Southwestern Company, 1966), page 544.

CHAPTER 2: SECRET PASSIONS—TWISTED, HONORABLE, OR HOLY?

1. Quoted from a cassette tape by Miss A. Wetherell Johnson from one of her Bible Study Fellowship lessons.

CHAPTER 3: I WANT TO FEEL SPECIAL

Opening quotation from Emily Dickinson, *The Complete Poems of Emily Dickinson,* Thomas H. Johnson ed., copyrighted in

1960 by Mary L. Hampson (Boston: Little, Brown and Company, 1960), page 133.

1. Francis Schaeffer, source unknown.
2. Ethel Barrett, *Don't Look Now, But Your Personality Is Showing* (Glendale, Calif.: Regal Division of Gospel Light Publications, 1968), page 3.
3. James Dobson, *What Wives Wish Their Husbands Knew About Women* (Wheaton, Ill.: Tyndale House Publishers, Inc., 1975), pages 22-23.
4. Gary Smalley and John Trent, *The Blessing* (Nashville: Thomas Nelson Publishers, 1986), page 24.
5. Sue Monk Kidd, *God's Joyful Surprise* (New York: Harper & Row Publishers, 1987), page 3.
6. Kidd, page 125.

CHAPTER 4: I WANT TO DO SOMETHING WORTHWHILE

1. Bruce Shelley, "Why Work," *Christianity Today,* July 14, 1987, page 16.
2. J. P. Moreland, "Work, the Good Life and the Great Commission," *Worldwide Challenge,* August 1988, page 57.
3. Raymond C. Ortlund, *Lord, Make My Life a Miracle* (Glendale, Calif.: Regal Books, 1974), pages 1-2.
4. Saint Augustine, *Confessions.*
5. John Piper, *Desiring God* (Portland, Oreg.: Multnomah Press, 1986), page 41.
6. Ellen Fielding, "Career Change," *Christianity Today,* December 11, 1987, page 27.
7. Ruth Tucker, "Working Mothers," *Christianity Today,* July 15, 1988, page 18.
8. Ralph Mattson and Arthur Miller, *Finding a Job You Can Love* (Nashville: Thomas Nelson Publishers, 1982), page 60.
9. Mattson and Miller, page 60.
10. Tim Hansel, *Holy Sweat* (Waco, Tex.: Word Books, 1987), page 36.
11. Bruce Larson quoted by Hansel pages, 36-37.

12. Elisabeth Elliot, *The Glory of God's Will* (Westchester, Ill.: Good News Publishers, 1982), no page.

CHAPTER 5: WHY ME? WHY THIS? WHY NOW?

1. Philip Yancey, *Disappointment with God* (Grand Rapids, Mich.: Zondervan Corporation, 1988), pages 44-46.
2. Chris Thurman, *The Lies We Believe* (Nashville: Thomas Nelson Publishers, 1989), pages 22, 24.
3. Stephen Olford quoted in a verbal presentation by Peg Rankin, Monmouth Beach, New Jersey.
4. Yancey, page 152.
5. Adapted from Larry Crabb, *Inside Out* (Colorado Springs, Colo.: NavPress, 1988), page 14.

CHAPTER 6: LORD, MAKE ME FLEXIBLE!

1. Richard Hooker, *Quotable Quotations,* compiled by Lloyd Cory (Wheaton, Ill.: Victor Books, 1985), page 54.
2. Jackie Hudson, *Doubt—A Road to Growth* (San Bernardino, Calif.: Here's Life Publishers, 1987), page 20.
3. Os Guinness, *In Two Minds* (Downers Grove, Ill.: InterVarsity Press, 1976), page 17.
4. Crabb, page 221.
5. Tim Hansel, *You Gotta Keep Dancin'* (Elgin, Ill.: David C. Cook Publisher, 1985), page 133.

CHAPTER 7: PLEASE HEAR ME!

1. Jan Fawcett, *Before It's Too Late,* prepared by the American Association of Suicidology (West Point, Penn.: Merek Sharp & Dohme), page 7.
2. Claire Safran, "Troubles That Pull Couples Apart," *Redbook,* January 1979, vol. 152, page 83.
3. Elisabeth Elliot, *Loneliness* (Nashville: Oliver-Nelson, 1988), back cover.
4. Alan McGinnis, *The Friendship Factor* (Minneapolis: Augsburg Publishing House, 1979), page 24.

5. C. S. Lewis, *The Four Loves,* quoted by Elisa Morgan, "Friendmaking," *Focal Point,* the quarterly of Denver Conservative Baptist Seminary.

CHAPTER 8: PLEASE HOLD ME!

1. Nanci Hellmich, "A Third of Women Rate Lovers a '10'," *USA Today,* July 13, 1988, page 4D.
2. The Editors, "How Common Is Pastoral Indiscretion?" *Leadership,* Winter 1988, vol. IX, no. 1, page 3.
3. Terri Schultz, "Does Marriage Give Women What They Really Want?" *Ladies Home Journal,* June 1980, page 90.
4. M. Scott Peck quoted by Robert J. Carlson, "Battling Sexual Indiscretion," *Ministry*, January 1987, pages 4-6.
5. Marshall Shelley, "From the Editors," *Leadership,* Winter 1988, vol. IX, no. 1, page 3.
6. Larson quoted by Carlson, page 4.
7. Ruth Senter, "Rick," *The Marriage Partnership,* January/February 1988, page 61.
8. Josh D. McDowell and Dick Day, *Why Wait? What You Need to Know About the Teen Sexuality Crisis* (San Bernardino, Calif.: Here's Life Publishers, 1987), page 318.
9. Walter Trobisch, *I Loved a Girl* (New York: Harper & Row Publishers, 1965), pages 3-4.

CHAPTER 9: I BLEW IT AGAIN!

1. Bob Benson, *Come Share the Being* (Nashville: Impact Books, 1974), pages 72-73.
2. Lois Mowday, *The Snare* (Colorado Springs, Colo.: NavPress, 1988), pages 55-56.
3. Yancey, page 106.

CHAPTER 10: SELF-ACTUALIZATION?

1. Paraphrased in part from Polly Redford, *Raccoons and Eagles: Two Views of American Wildlife* (New York: E. P. Dutton, 1965), page 191.

2. M. Scott Peck, *The Road Less Traveled: A New Psychology of Love, Traditional Values and Spiritual Growth* (New York: Simon and Shuster, 1978), page 44.
3. Thurman, page 58.
4. Al Janssen, *Choices for Graduates* (Grand Rapids, Mich.: Baker Book House, 1988), page 26.
5. Madeleine L'Engle quoted by Janssen, page 28.

CHAPTER 11: WHATEVER THE ABUNDANT LIFE IS, I WANT IT!

1. Francis Schaeffer, *True Spirituality* (Wheaton, Ill.: Tyndale House Publishers, 1971), page 3.
2. Rusty Rustenbach, "What Do You Expect?" *Discipleship Journal,* issue 53, 1989, page 59.
3. Rustenbach, pages 59-60.
4. R. C. Sproul, "Table Talk," Ligonier Ministries, February 1989, page 14.

CHAPTER 12: ME—GOD'S WOMAN?

1. Cliff Barrows, quoted from a tribute in *Corrie ten Boom: Clippings from My Notebook* (Minneapolis: World Wide Publications, 1984), page 3.
2. J. Oswald Sanders, *Spiritual Leadership* (Chicago: Moody Press, 1967), page 40.
3. Frank Minirth quoted in the foreword of Thurman.
4. Ruth Senter, "The Bittersweet of Letting Go," *Today's Christian Woman,* September/October 1989, page 43.

CAROL KENT MINISTRIES

In addition to conference and retreat speaking, Carol Kent presents "Speak Up With Confidence" seminars in many cities each year. The seminars are designed to train Christians to communicate more effectively. Presented in a three-day format, participants learn how to find and use illustrations, how to gain the attention of an audience, how to organize and file speaking material, and how to overcome stage fright.

For more information on Carol's cassette tapes, "Speak Up" seminars, or for details related to scheduling her to speak in your area, contact:

Carol Kent Ministries
P.O. Box 610941
Port Huron, Michigan 48061-0941
(810) 982-0898
(810) 987-4163: fax